Language and Typography

Cal Swann

Lund Humphries, London

Copyright ©1991 Cal Swann

First edition 1991
Published by Lund Humphries Publishers Ltd
16 Pembridge Road, London W11

Designed by Cal Swann

British Cataloguing in Publication Data
Swann, Cal
Language and Typography
1. Typography. Linguistic aspects
1. Title
686.22
ISBN 0 85331 570 1

Typesetting by LeType LeArt Pty Ltd,
Adelaide South Australia

Made and printed in Great Britain

This book is dedicated to Luke Martin Swann

Acknowledgements

It is customary to absolve one's helpers from any critical blame that might be ascribed to the contents of a book and this duty I duly perform. At the same time, without the encouragement and willing advice given by so many people, I would not have completed this project, so that my gratitude is heartfelt.

Without Mary Wood's push in quite a specific direction and towards an independent study of language, I would not have met all the excellent and helpful staff at Lancaster University's Linguistics Department, and especially Professor Christopher Candlin and David Barton who helped enormously in my preparatory work at the University.

I am particularly indebted to John Taylor for making the text more readable. In quite practical ways, Arthur Linacre and Rex Edwards accomplished various production tasks, and, above all, Pat MacHenry fought long and hard with the word processor – and won. My thanks are also extended to my colleagues in Australia namely Keith Goldsworthy, Rob Pilcher, Stuart Gluth, Danuta Kuczera and Martin Rowe who provided crucial help with the drawings.

In addition to those above who have helped with the writing and production of this book are all those companies who have allowed me to use examples of their work, and to them I extend my gratitude. In particular, Fig 21 from the Stifts-Bibliothek of St Gallen in Switzerland and Fig 22 from the British Library in London. Not least, my thanks are due to the individuals who have given me their photographs, words or designs; Phil Baines, Alan Brickwood, Alistair Cooke, Don Hatcher, Hans Lutz, David Sless, Bev Staley and Karl Swann.

Finally, my thanks to Birthe who, in her easy-going way, firmly locked me in my room until I finished each section.

Contents

Introduction

10 *Chapter 1 – Introduction to language as human communication*
This chapter defines the word language and introduces linguistic terminology in pointing out some of the main characteristics of the spoken language. The link is then made between the verbal and visual signals we use in conjunction with language as a method of human communication, and concludes with a brief look at some basic communication theory.

23 *Chapter 2 – A developing and living language*
This is a brief summary of how the English Language developed into an accepted standard with particular reference to the role of the written/printed word. It touches upon the variability of English as a living language and explores some of the differences of expression according to the purpose and media by which the language is transmitted.

31 *Chapter 3 – The visual system*
This chapter looks at the visual transmission of language as typography and outlines some of the research into factors affecting legibility. It establishes the visual perception of language as a cognitive route to understanding distinct from the aural route. It then outlines some of the structural categories by which the visible language may be transmitted.

54 *Chapter 4 – Form and connotation*
This explores the complexity of the relationship between content, form and context. It considers the shape of the letters, their connotative qualities, and how these factors are further influenced by aesthetics, size and general layout. The complementary relationship of function and form are examined in a number of conventional visual registers.

75 *Chapter 5 – Visible speech?*
This chapter looks at a number of amateur and professional productions of public signs in an examination of their linguistic content, visual presentation, and ethnographic context. It first indicates that public understanding of both aural and visual language areas is very basic and ultimately inadequate, and demonstrates this by looking at the varied quality of some of the signs and notices produced in the environment. It then suggests a general approach to the analysis of the language and layout of signs and advertisements and examines a particular example as a case study. Finally, a brief review of the ground covered in these chapters.

95 *Bibliography*

The craft of typography has traditionally involved the arrangement of single units of metal type to form words, sentences, lines and paragraphs to print on a sheet of paper. The mechanical constraints of this process imposed a discipline which, combined with imagination, resulted in the printed page being attractive and legible for the reader. The majority of designers who deal with typography have usually learned this craft through exercises in the visual manipulation of letterforms based on an understanding (if not the practice) of the metal discipline. The craft of writing, in particular the writing of copy for the media, has usually been learned or acquired as an entirely separate activity and used by journalists, editors and advertising copywriters, etc. These two distinct areas often come together in practice as there is clearly a very strong relationship between the conception of the words as a message and their transmission in visible form.

Today's technology has magically rendered the means of composing words much more accessible and virtually anyone can now conjure up sophisticated typefaces at the touch of a button. What is important is what is said and how it is seen. The phrase 'who says what to whom with what effect' has even greater significance to the message-makers. This book is an introduction to the basic concepts about the primary language as a spoken/aural system and the transmission of a visible language system which has some important differences from as well as similarities to the spoken version.

In seeking to bring the two crafts together – the craft of writing and the craft of typography – this does not attempt to be a how-to-do-it book but a description of language and typography in practical usage, with the intention of improving the understanding of the processes involved. The introduction of linguistic terminology is intended to bridge the gap between the designer/writers and the analysts of messages in the media, enabling more fruitful discourse to take place between the two groups. Greater understanding of what the practitioners and the commentators are saying from their respective viewpoints would be helpful in tackling future problems of communication where a collaborative effort could achieve more effective and purposive messages.

The book is intended for students of design and language and all those who seek an opening into either or both of the two fields. Linguists are likely to skip chapters one and two, and the more experienced designers will find chapter three, in particular, very familiar territory. There is a bibliography at the back of this book, but at the end of each chapter I have included some recommendations for further reading from some of the books which as a designer, I have found useful and interesting. This book is an introduction and nothing more, and if it stimulates the reader to seek out more detailed information from the immense range of linguistic and design books which are currently available, this one will have served a useful purpose.

What is language ?

In common usage, language is often made to refer to a variety of interpretations such as the language of love or language of drawing. Like many words, it is borrowed as a metaphor from its literal meaning and applied in different contexts to embellish a new interpretation. Such variations may enrich the colour of the discourse, but they sometimes serve to blur the original meaning. In its strictest sense, language is the system of sound signals which the human animal uses in highly structured arrangements. Language is not as effective as the theoretical concept of thought transference, but it is the most sophisticated system we have for the transmission of complex ideas. Over 5,000 variations exist in the world and despite the problems of multi-interpretations, it is the next best thing to Extra-Sensory-Perception and is arguably the most important tool available to enable human beings to control the environment.

Animals use sound and sight signals to communicate quite basic information about their instincts and immediate surroundings. Some threaten with growls, while others whistle at the approach of danger or perform a ritual dance as a prelude to mating. The ritual dance or the warning bark is almost always the same and is very restricted in the amount or subtlety of information given.

The important difference between animal and human vocal signals is in the structure and arrangement. Dolphins, chimpanzees and gorillas can make between 20 and 30 different sounds, cows a mere 10 and chickens in the region of 30. The human animal is endowed with vocal equipment which is capable of a similar range of sounds, but it is not the capacity which makes the difference. It is the organisation and infinitely variable combinations which make the human language system so superior and distinctive from the rest.

Fig 1

Mmmmmmmmmmmmmm . . .

Shshshsh . .

Ouch!

The 40–45 distinctive sounds which an English-speaker uses (some languages use more, some as little as 15) represent the vowels and consonants, and these make up the smallest units (phonemes) of our language system. These phonemes form words and sentences when structured within the framework of a language system. Unstructured sounds can still have meaning (Fig 1) but it is the amalgamation of the small sound units into larger units within a certain pattern that gives meaning to the signals and enables enormously complex messages to be transmitted. Three simple sounds: 'd' 'o' 'g' are meaningless in themselves, but when put together as 'dog', represent the English word for a domestic animal. The same three sounds in reverse order 'god' represent a different concept. The structure of phonemes into words (phonology and morphology) and the structure of words into sentences (syntax) imparts meaning (semantics) in a language system.

The structure of a language is the grammar of the language and although grammar varies from one language to another it is always made up of the three elements of phonology, syntax and semantics (Fig 2). The grammatical rules are often broken, especially in the spoken version, but the basic pattern is always present. The breaking of the rules is usually because of a common oral tradition or is sometimes a deliberate tactic by a speaker to make a particular point. Although learners of a language will often make simple mistakes in selecting the correct ending to a word (to make it plural, or masculine, etc), the underlying pattern of a language is ever present and is why we know that 'gdo' or 'dgo' isn't a word.

Human language is quite arbitrary. The sounds have no meaning in themselves (with the exception of a few onomatopoeic words such as 'bang', or 'snap', 'crackle' and 'pop') and whatever meaning is placed upon a sound is entirely dependent upon the speech community. The word 'bang' is a representational sound whereas 'dog' or 'cat' are symbolic sounds which stand in English for particular things. The sound symbols have to be learned and are not inherited as are the cries of animals.

Fig 2

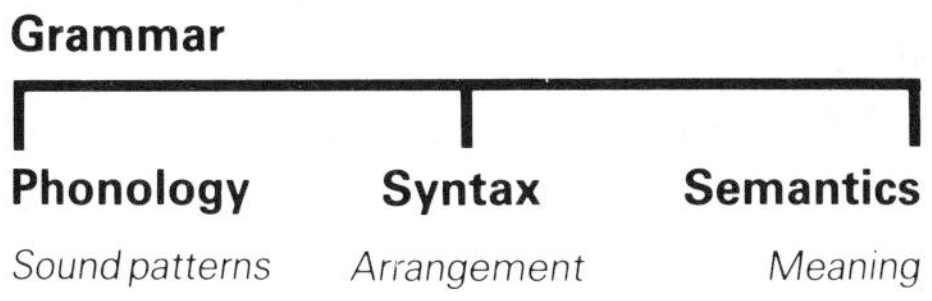

Grammar

Phonology	**Syntax**	**Semantics**
Sound patterns	*Arrangement*	*Meaning*

It is generally believed that the human animal possesses some innate language facility, but it has to be developed over a fairly lengthy learning period. The inarticulate babble of a baby (see Fig 3 – in this case, the author's version of baby talk taken from his design for his son's birth announcement) will develop into English or Chinese, according to the speech community in which it lives. The ability of a child to embrace a language is quite extraordinary and it is common for children of mixed speech communities to acquire a multi-lingual facility with ease.

The sounds produced and heard by one spee community may not be understood by anoth Each community develops a language system which is appropriate for its environment and culture. English-speakers will often comment on the number of words which the Eskimo h for snow, but for the English climate, terms such as 'drizzle', 'mist', 'shower', 'sleet', 'downpour' etc, serve a similar purpose, denoting subtle descriptions of rain, which are unknown to sunnier cultures. A national culture is comprised of many sub-cultures and within a single speech community there can be considerable gaps which result in non-communication between social classes c groups. The sign 'JC4U' (Fig 4) is meaningles without the visual context of the church (Fig and the sub-cultural knowledge that 'JC' stan for Jesus Christ and '4U' can be read as for yc

Fig 3

"Waaaagagh! Yeoooowueee! Mamaahag! Boowooyuuph! Wighoo! Hee-hee-ha!"

The arbitrary nature of the language system, with its infinitely variable units, accounts for its endless creativity. Humans invent new sounds and make up new words which constantly enrich the language and add new meanings to words by new associations. Shakespeare invented many new words and is thought to have had a vocabulary of over 30,000 words, about twice as many as the average educated speaker of today. A number of writers (Joyce, Dahl, etc) have enjoyed inventing new words (neologisms) and poets, like advertising copywriters, are especially allowed freedom to play with words and phrases within the conventions of their crafts.

We think in terms of language and having a language structure enables us to develop thinking into action. The interconnection between thinking and the articulation of thought is inextricable and language-dependent. Marshall Mcluhan (among others) went further and described 'typographic man' as a more intellectual human being who was able to develop rational thinking through being literate following the advent of the recorded word in writing/printing. This commonly held view is contested by those who subscribe to the view that oral cultures have alternative systems to articulate explicit ideas and that no evidence exists to show that writing/printing cultures have superior thought processes. What is not in doubt is that thinking takes place by making use of a language and many support the Sapir-Whorf hypothesis which states that the way people view the world is conditioned by their native language and that this dominates their thinking.

Fig 4

Fig 5

The growth of language

We have no way of knowing how our ancestors started to use the sound-signalling system in any sophisticated sense that would equate to a language, but it is likely that it was developing at least as fast as the making of the first flint tools and would have been highly developed by the time of the existence of a culture which could paint elaborate hunting images on cave walls. It is generally believed that western languages evolved from a Euro/Asian base and some geographical/national segments can be easily recognised (Fig 6), but what started it all remains a mystery.

Various theories have been offered which usually rely upon the need for group co-ordination as the stimulus for developme[n]t. The involuntary gasp which we make when lifting or pushing a heavy item, for example, may have resulted in some eventual coding of a co-ordinated 'Heave-Ho'. Perhaps the extraordinary manipulation of the facial muscles (Fig 7), especially the elasticated mouth, is part of the story, as gesture is stron[gly] linked with language and communication. The development of language is well covere[d] elsewhere (see bibliography), but the connection between the visual signals which provide the context within which oral signal[s] are uttered and received is the theme of this book, and it is worth exploring some aspect[s] at this basic level.

Fig 6

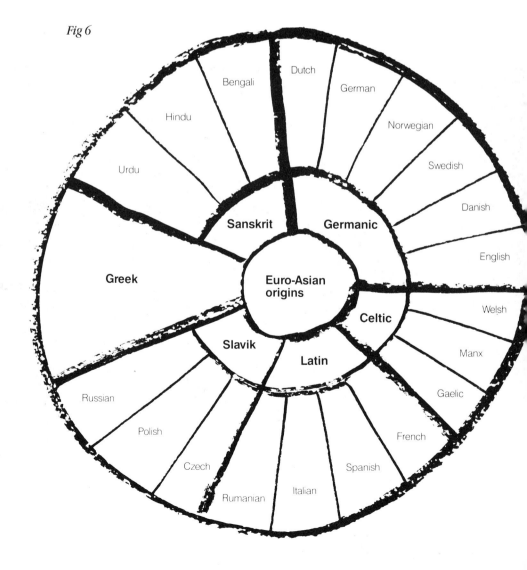

The human face is unique in its facility to display such a wide variety of expressions. The hands too have been freed from other duties and frequently support verbal communication with gestures which are largely derived from the cultural context. The human animal also uses body language in either direct or unwitting postures which communicate additional information (sometimes in contrast!) to the verbal message. The face, however, is capable of a number of primary expressions which are inborn and universal (Figs 8 & 9) and which are directly related to communication of emotions or stages of condition.

Smiling, laughing, crying, etc are primary gestures and send messages to another human being, and many utterances are delivered with the non-verbal signal of a smile etc. Such accompaniment may be entirely supportive of the basic message, or used to soften an admonishment which may otherwise be too harsh.

Fig 7

Fig 8

Fig 9

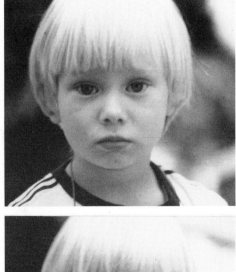

The eyes and mouth are the clearest indications of the conditions under which an oral message is being sent and any speaker is watched carefully in the listeners' attempts to receive the true message. Facial expressions have been formalised and decorated in ritual situations in all communities from the Bilas cosmetic of the New Guinea girl (Fig 10) to the special signals of tribal warpaint.

The symbolism of facial expressions is used i many visual situations by designers and even simple curved line can be very recognisable a a smile, or a face with a tear from the eye is used to signify sorrow (Fig 11).

Fig 10

Fig 11

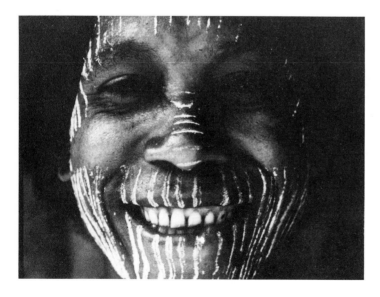

These are often direct signs which are representational and sometimes indirect signs which have a particular meaning within one culture context (and have different meanings in different cultures, Fig 12).

Signs which have become codified and depend on learning are like a form of language. They are symbols which are arbitrary and stand for something other than themselves in the way that 'd' 'o' 'g' or 'c' 'h' 'i' 'e' 'n' stands for an animal (Fig 13). A drawing of a dog is a representational sign (Fig 14) whereas the surrounding circle with a bar across it is a symbol like the arbitrary signs of the alphabet (Fig 15).

Fig 13

**dog
chien
hund
cane**

Fig 14

Fig 15

The development of writing incorporated the use of symbolic drawing which at first represented things in picture-writing (hieroglyphics or sacred scripts) and then sounds. The alphabet developed into a very formal code representing sounds which we have to learn in order to decode.

There are many codes in existence which require greater or lesser degrees of learning, with some of the easier ones being visual systems closely related to primary visual sign which are also representational, (Figs 16 & 17)

Fig 16a

Fig 16b

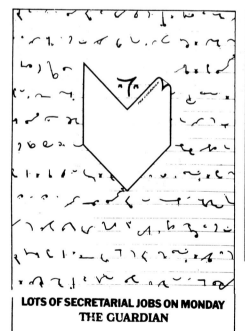

LOTS OF SECRETARIAL JOBS ON MONDAY THE GUARDIAN

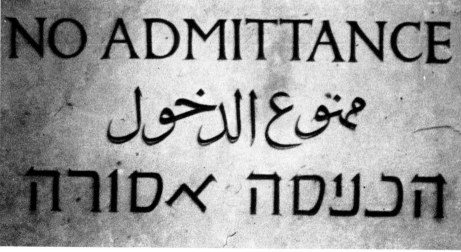

The communication process and codes

Language is a central feature in the communication process, particularly in transmitting abstract or complex ideas. In order to understand further the whole area of verbal and non-verbal elements in this process it is necessary to examine the nature of the activity we regard as communication, itself a much abused and over-used word.

Communication theory has developed during the past 50 years and has been articulated and studied as an academic discipline. There are two main definitions which are generally seen to be at extreme ends of a spectrum. Broadly, one view is that communication has taken place when a message has been sent from a source by some means, and a recipient has received it. The assumption is that the sender has expressed the message correctly and that the receiver has decoded it with the intended interpretation. This one-way process is sometimes referred to as manipulative communication.

The second view is that communication is a participative process and that an intended message is only communicated when the receiver shares with the sender the cultural interpretative values inherent in the signals themselves, and interacts accordingly. In between these two poles are many shades of emphasis: the one-way definition may have more relevance in the area of media communication, whereas the participative view may be more appropriate in face-to-face situations where interaction is expected to take place.

Fig 17a

Fig 17b

Fig 17c

The first (and now classic) model of the communication process was produced by Shannon and Weaver in 1949 (Fig 18). These two engineers originated their theories from working with mechanical communication processes but they were quick to apply their model to the field of human systems. Their definition of an informative source encoding a message, which is then transmitted along a channel to a receiver, who then decodes the message and reacts in some way, has provided the basis for many subsequent models.

The Shannon and Weaver model stresses the linear process of a message travelling from A B and relies heavily on the notion that provid the channel is clear and free from interferenc (the inclusion of noise in the diagram is easil understood when we know that their origina work was with telephone systems), then the message will be accurately decoded. It does not show the important effects that feedback and the social psychological context have on all the stages in the process, especially at sour and receiver. A revised Shannon and Weaver diagram (Fig 19) might show the overall socia context and the sub-cultures at source and receiving ends. Without some shared experience in these sub-cultures, communication may not occur.

Shannon & Weaver 1949

Fig 18

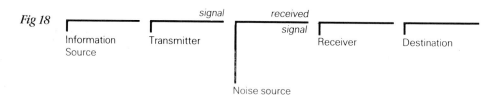

Fig 19

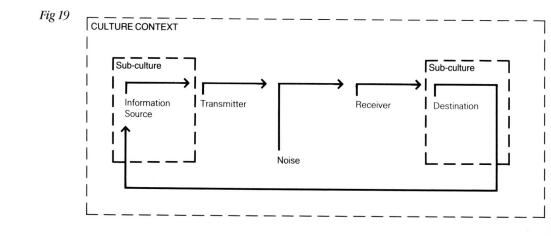

Later models (notably Gerbner, Berlo, et al) have attempted to illustrate the participative theory which takes into account the way the message is perceived by the reader, the cultural context, and the form of signals which make up the message, etc. The diagram below (Fig 20) illustrates something of the relationship of language in both oral and visual processes of communication.

Communication occurs on many levels by various, and usually a multiplicity of, channels from a source to a receiver. Most of the human senses are in use during the process, but principally sight and sound. Language is part of the package. Sometimes seen more than heard and always interpreted according to the context. Communication is culture-dependent and often a listener can understand what is being communicated by the gestures and situation, without being familiar with the speaker's language. The context can be coloured by the speaker's intention and prowess in the media, so that the receiver has to work hard at the interpretation. The process is very complex but we start to learn the strategies from the very first cry.

Fig 20

The classic work on the evolution of the English language is Barber's *The Story of Language.* This is a readable book – particularly the first half – which is clear and to the point but covers in some detail the whole evolution and spread of language. It is English/European based and concentrates on the period up to Early Modern English.

A more recent and less academic book is *The Story of English* which arose from the TV series of the same title. This is an excellently illustrated and very wide-ranging survey of the growth and diversity of the English language throughout the world. As a popularist book on language it contains very little linguistic terminology and with its strong transatlantic flavour, a useful introduction for designers to the different cultural associations which can be derived from a common language.

For those who seek an introduction to linguistics, Jean Aitchison's (UK) book of that title is well worth acquiring, if only for Parts One and Two. It clearly sets out the territory and employs simple language for what can be highly technical or academically intimidating to visually orientated people. Almost any of Aitchison's publications are recommended as she has an easy and personal style which is sprinkled liberally with imaginative examples that demonstrate her ideas. Especially fascinating is *The Articulate Mammal* which should be read by every would-be communicator. Her opening chapters on 'Animals that try to talk' are stimulating enough to keep the design reader interested throughout the more linguistic content further on. Worth mentioning here too is her *Language Change: Progress or Decay?* which is an in-depth study of the ground covered in my next chapter. However, her observations on how languages begin, change and die (Part 4) are particularly illuminating.

Dwight Bolinger (USA), in addition to being an eminent linguist, is also an excellent communicator and his books are all very readable. *Aspects of Language* (Bolinger & Sears) is a particularly good introduction to t▌ field of linguistics and chapters 1 and 8 enou▌ to start the design reader. *Language, the Loaded Weapon* has much to offer the copywriter and designer as the title might suggest. Chapters 1, 2, 5 and 6 should be enough to whet the appetite and copywriters▌ especially should read Chapter 9 on sexism .

Communication studies is a comparatively recent academic discipline and an increasing number of books are coming on the market. Probably the standard introduction is Fiske's *Introduction to Communication Studies* which spells out in very clear order the basic principles and summarises the many models and theories which have developed. *See What I Mean* has been produced by two authors drawn from the world of linguistics and of artist/designer respectively. Clearly designed to bridge the gap, it is a primer aime▌ at art and design students and is an easy introduction to a theoretical understanding of visual communication. John Berger's work on perception are very relevant to this arena and so is that of the anthropologist Desmond Morris. In addition to his *Manwatching* serie▌ *Gestures* offers an interesting perspective on culture and communication.

Towards a standard language

Language has been developing for about a million years and the evolution of national languages even in the generalised form represented by the diagram (Fig 6) is a comparatively recent event. This development is better covered elsewhere, but a brief summary of trends which have influenced and been influenced by the advent of the visible transmission of the language in written or printed form, is worth attempting in the context of this book.

The English language has been a hybrid of many influxes and reached a state of what is termed 'modern English' a little after the invention of printing towards the end of the fifteenth century. What might be termed standard English or BBC English is not much more than a hundred years old, and evolution of the English language is ongoing.

The notion of one ideal is a comparatively recent concept and is confined to a small number of language cultures (particularly English and French). Speakers of English from different parts of Britain during the Middle Ages would have had some difficulty in understanding one another's regional spoken variation, and scribes wrote their manuscripts in a local script using spellings that reflected their own regional pronunciation. When William Caxton set up the first printing press in Britain (1476) he complained of the lack of a standard orthography and dialect which would be understood by all. In actual fact, a standard pronunciation together with a more standardised written form was beginning to emerge by then and the introduction of printing hastened the process of disseminating this standard.

Towards the end of the Middle Ages it was the East Midlands regional dialect which was beginning to emerge as a dominant form. From the Midlands to East Anglia a prosperous wool trade had developed and the commercial centre for business dealings for the region and the continent was London. Successful merchants, men of influence and political power at Court, were often speakers of the Midlands vernacular, or were at least influenced by it. This dominant business accent was to become (in modified form), the accepted pronunciation for Court and government and later became the London/South East dialect.

The Roman alphabet had by then been developed from the capital letters of the Roman era (Fig 21) to a system which combined capitals and lower-case minuscule letters (Fig 22). Latin had survived as the language of the written word in Europe for over 1,000 years and men of learning were able to read Latin texts irrespective of their native spoken language. From the ninth century onwards a surge of nationalistic feelings had stimulated the growth of books written in local vernaculars. King Alfred was the first scholar to translate Latin writings into English. The Lindisfarne Gospels written in Latin around 700AD (Fig 22) shows an Anglo-Saxon translation added between the lines (by the priest Aldred) in the tenth century.

The introduction of the printing press in Europe had two interesting effects. On the one hand it hastened the demise of Latin as an international language of learning by fulfilling the demands of individual nations to make more books available in their national vernacular. At the same time, the increased quantity and ready availability of one printed vernacular style hastened the demise of regional variations within the national boundaries.

Fig 21

In the absence of a recognised spoken or written standard, the early printers made their own decisions. Caxton and a number of his contemporaries learned the craft of printing in the Netherlands and some English words such as 'yot' became 'yacht'; there are numerous other examples of irregular spellings which occurred quite arbitrarily but have become standard due to the permanence of print. Caxton's successor, Wynkyn de Worde, pursued Caxton's conscious efforts to create a standard and although he took texts from prior generations of authors, he altered the original spellings to conform to the new standard. In effect, Wynkyn initiated the modern publisher's practice of having an established 'House Style' which launders out the variability of individual authors' scripts.

With the gradual establishment of a Standard English in a selected dialect (and a standard printed form), came the notion that deviation from the spoken norm was somehow inferior. It was not long before social values were then applied to those who spoke the standard and those who spoke the 'rustic' variety – whatever that might be. By the end of the sixteenth century this difference was being seen as an indicator of social standing and education. Stereotyping of non-standard speakers was being employed by writers and entertainers to cast them as buffoons or simple-minded ruffians.

The process of codification was eventually carried out in the eighteenth century by a small group of scholars, such as Samuel Johnson and his influential *Dictionary* and in the United States by Noah Webster in the nineteenth century. This entailed the selection of a particular variety and its promotion, with elaborate rules of grammar, as the acceptable standard.

Fig 22

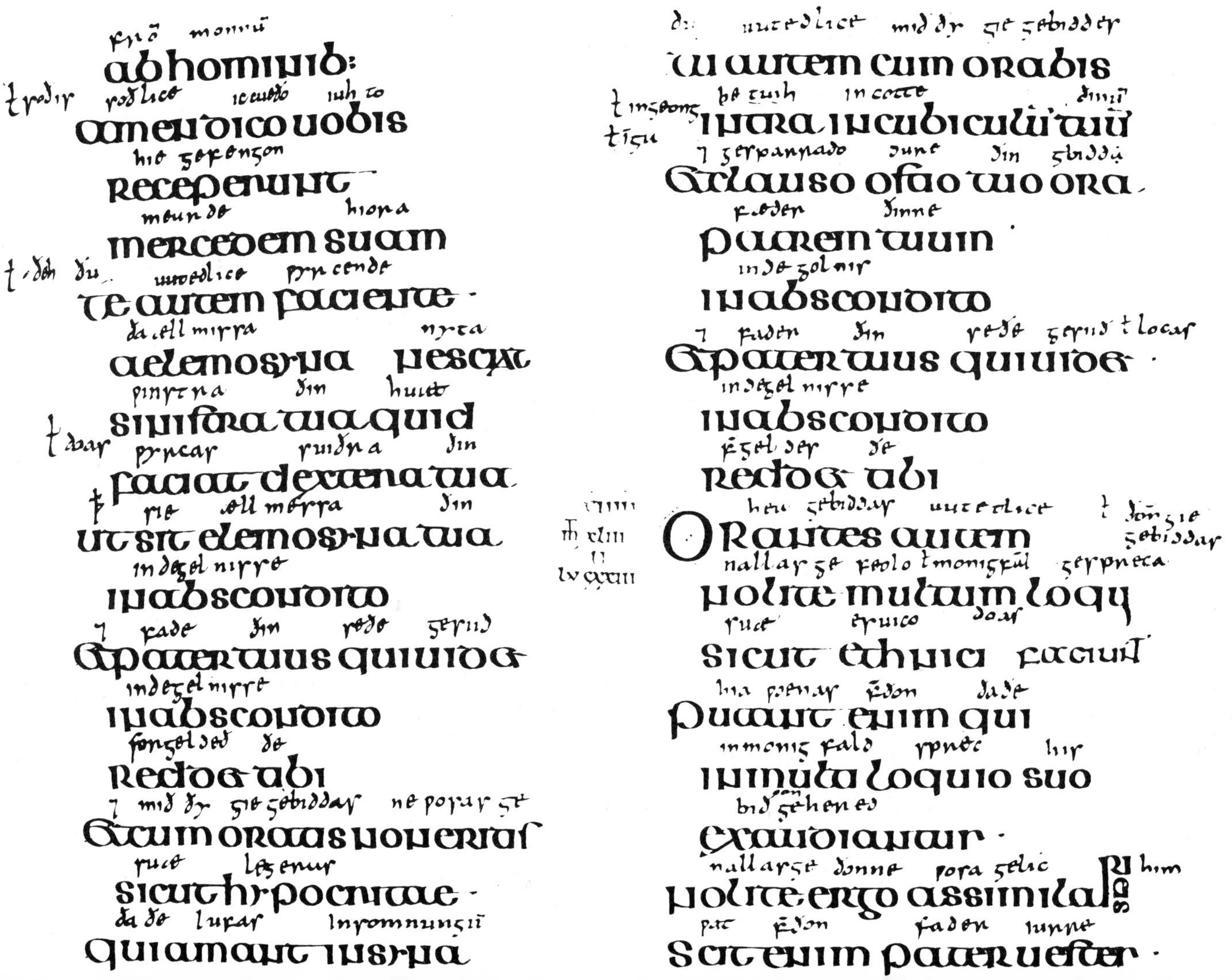

This process set forth an era of prescriptive declarations about the English language, its correct usage in both spoken and written forms. The lexicographers and grammarians, however, were faced with innumerable difficulties, as the inheritance of so many arbitrary spellings, which had become accepted standards, did not fall easily into a system such as that of Latin. The mix of Celtic, Anglo-Saxon, Viking, Norman-French et al, which had produced a rich English language made all the richer by inventive writers such as Chaucer, Spencer and Shakespeare, left a language which it was difficult to codify. The scholars who set about this task were inevitably Latin scholars and as Latin was no longer a spoken language, it therefore appeared to be a fixed and well-regulated written model which could be applied to codify English. Traditional English phrases such as 'it's me' were considered incorrect as the Latin construction 'ego sum' used the subject pronoun 'ego' rather than the object 'me'. Good English therefore should be 'it is I'. Most speakers still say 'it's me', but our present-day grammatical rules specify a Latin-based formula for this and many other forms as a 'correct' version.

The efforts of the scholars to impose a 'rational' code, and their obsession with etymology as the key to fixing the language in an approved form, were contrary to the natural flux of a living language. We use the spoken language overwhelmingly more than we use the written form, and the 'fixity of print' cannot contain the natural changes which constantly occur in the spoken variety, since these are 'beyond the control of school teachers or governments'. Control could only be exercised over a very small section of the community, through a co-ordinated effort of schooling, parental/family pressure and a closed social system. The prescriptive doctrines of the learned men of the eighteenth century became the specialised language form for the few who could exercise such tight control, the educated rich and powerful. By the end of the nineteenth century, the public schools which in Britain educated the young for this section of the community, were the breeding-ground for the kind of English pronunciation which was received in 'proper' society. This form of pronunciation, which was associated with the speech of less than 4 per cent of the British population, became symbolic of authority and power.

Variations of the standard

The universal acknowledgement of an RP (Received Pronunciation) accent as the 'correct' way of speaking, which was reinforced by BBC broadcasts throughout the world during the 1930s and the Second World War, began to decline again in Britain with the popularity of regional dialects spoken (among others) by a number of actors portraying 'real life' dramas on radio and television. More significant was the importance of American English, which from the Second World War onwards became the worldwide language of power and authority. The post-war export from the United States of films, television soap operas and made-for-TV-movies, made the Hollywood glamour and American accent even more accessible to an English-speaking world.

The anglification of many parts of the world, prior to the establishment of a standard pronunciation, left the way clear for several variations of the English language to develop and mature. There are social values attached to particular accents (as opposed to those which are usually defined as 'uneducated' or 'rural') in all the Western cultures, but there is undoubtedly greater flexibility in vocabulary (and to a lesser extent in spelling) in the non-UK versions of English. The Americans and Australians especially like to coin new words and phrases and this cultural disposition continues to enrich an ever-changing language. A typical example is the American invention of 'yuppie' (derived from 'young/upward/professional') and it is interesting to note how quickly it became absorbed into the common language around the world (Fig 23).

Fig 23

Language registers

The customs and values that are held by a community are being adjusted constantly. These adjustments are expressed in the language and a different outlook by a new generation will make quite major changes in the vocabulary and tone of the voice (Fig 24). Similar changes are made by different sectors of a community when each will use a special set of words and phrases (registers) which have become conventions within those sectors. The specialist language of legal affairs, the scientist (Fig 25), the educationalist or the computer expert are obvious examples. Less well recognised is the switching from one register to another which we all perform in our daily discourse. There are different registers for work, home or play and many skilled communicators will have a wide range of registers to apply in appropriate situations. The intuitive adjustment that speakers make when addressing a particular group of listeners, such as a group of ten-year-old children, becomes a highly refined and conscious pitch when professional speech-writers or advertising copywriters are designing their language strategies.

Choosing the appropriate register is normally semi-conscious reaction to the speech situation. A speaker will be well aware that addressing a large committee meeting requires a very different presentation to the informal pressing of the same argument with a few colleagues over a drink. Similarly the committee presentation may even have been part-structured by notes made while other speakers were taking their turn in the debate. This aide memoire available to typographic cultures is certainly an extra tool which enables a speaker to keep track of the points that are being elaborated through the improvised spoken word. Highly gifted performers of improvised speech such as comedians, after-dinner speakers and orators, etc, are able to string together a series of engaging stories into a coherent whole, but the more serious the social situation and importance of the message the more structured and considered must be the choice of words.

Fig 24

> a very good thing for fathers to be present at the births of their children.
>   The announcement at 11 am yesterday said: "It is announced from Buckingham Palace that the Princess of Wales is expecting a baby in June next year" — a contrast from 1947, when the announcement simply read: "Her Royal Highness, the Princess Elizabeth, Duchess of Edinburgh, will undertake no public engagements after the end of June."
>   The Princess is likely to

Fig 25

Inositol-(1,4,5)-trisphosphate and calcium release at fertilization in sea-urchin eggs

By Karl Swann*. *Department of Physiology, University College London*

At fertilization in sea-urchin eggs the vitelline membrane is elevated as a result of the exocytosis of cortical granules. The membrane elevation moves as a wave from the point of sperm entry to the opposite side of the egg and is thought to result from an underlying wave of calcium release which activates the egg. Microinjection of Inositol-(1,4,5)-trisphosphate ($InsP_3$) can activate eggs and cause an autocatalytic wave of membrane elevation. It is thought to release calcium ions from intracellular stores. Microinjection of 5 pl (1 % egg volume) of buffered solutions (480 mM-KCl, 20 mM-PIPES, 100 μM-EGTA, pH 6·7) containing 1 μM-$InsP_3$ into unfertilized eggs (*Lytechinus pictus*) caused a complete membrane elevation (10/10 eggs). Inclusion of higher concentrations of the calcium chelator ethylene-bis-β-(aminoethylether)-N,N'-tetraacetic acid (EGTA) in the injection buffer (100 mM-EGTA, 8 EGTA replacing KCl, mol for mol) inhibited membrane elevation in response to $InsP_3$ (membrane elevation in 0/10 eggs), supporting the hypothesis that $InsP_3$ activates eggs by releasing calcium from internal stores.

Through the technology of broadcasting, a speaker may have a national or global audience and knowing how the message will be received by such diverse recipients is both difficult and important. The wrong words, or deviations from a prepared script to improvised speech, can have disastrous consequences, as many politicians have discovered. Pre-planning or designing a message which is appropriate for the receiver and the channel of communication is succinctly explained by Alistair Cooke in his preface to the 1979 publication of *The Americans*, which was originally a series of radio broadcasts, then converted into book form:

" The word 'reader' ought to be in strong italics. For these are talks meant to be listened to. And the job of writing – and then performing – a radio talk has been for me, down forty-odd years, by far the most challenging and satisfying craft of any I have attempted in a lifetime of journalism.

The challenge is not to write for your friends, or the intelligentsia, or your newspaper editor, but for an audience that spans the human gamut in very many countries. For these weekly thirteen-and-a-half minute talks were broadcast first in the Home Service of the British Broadcasting Corporation and then aired, through the overseas service of the BBC, on every continent (they can be heard in the United States only on the short wave). It is a great privilege to have the ear, at least the opportunity to entice the ear, of ordinary people and extraordinary people in countries as far apart as Scotland and Malaysia. I stress the unique satisfaction of the medium because nothing could be more rewarding than the sort of letter which acknowledges that a German grocer has been touched by an obituary piece on Dean Acheson or a Lord Chief Justice moved by the story of an illiterate black girl who swiped a baby from the incubator of a New York hospital.

Radio is literature for, so to speak, the blind. For one friend sitting in a room, not for any large collective audience that might be assembled in Madison Square Garden. And because the 'one friend in a room' may be of any colour, any station in life, any sort of education, the radio talker must try to write in an idiom acceptable to almost everybody who normally speaks the language. There are vocabularies, such as you could write for your newspaper or for a serious periodical, which are taboo as talk. Ideally, one ought to be Daniel Defoe, or John Bunyan, or Pepys, or Mark Twain, or the Jacobean translators of the Book of Genesis. This is, of course, an almost impossible challenge, and it is rarely met and conquered. Consequently, in going over these talks for publication I have made the most of the privilege of print to straighten out the syntax (which one doesn't do in conversation) and to introduce occasionally literary words that are more exact and that will not throw the much smaller race of book-readers. "

Language arose in face-to-face encounters in either single or small group situations and direct communication was limited to the distance the human voice could carry until the development of writing. The transmission of language in a visible form allowed a speaker's message to be heard by receivers at a distance of space and time. The invention of printing enlarged that process enormously and current technology provides a multitude of recording and transmission methods which exercises the language in manifold strategies and effects. In this domain of multi-media channels it is important for the message-makers to understand the qualities which are inherent in the spoken language, and the overlapping or major differences in the transmission of the language in alternative (and often parallel) channels of transmission. The conversion of the sound signals into visual signals is what we now refer to under the various titles of written, typographic, visible, or graphic language. The nature of these transmission channels entails pre-planning, and designing the most appropriate form requires a detailed understanding of the orthographic (written/printed) system.

My chapter is a mere skirmish into a fascinating history of language development and change. It serves to illustrate how rapidly changes can be affected in a spoken language and the haphazard but subsequently more permanent impact of the recorded visible language. A number of the books in the list at the end have devoted a section or so to historical development, and *The Story of English* treats it with clarity and interest. For readers who would like to pursue this topic in some depth, Dick Leith's *A Social History of English* is comprehensive and a very interesting study of the development of English in the British Isles.

If you can find a copy in the library, Steinberg's *500 Years of Printing* (1955), gives a succinct history during Chapter 1 of the early printers' efforts to contain a vernacular language in recorded form. There are very few publications which have covered the relationship between the developing language and its printed form and it is an area which is worthy of more research. *Language and Literacy* (Stubbs) is a more detailed analysis of the language in its spoken and written forms. Part Two is particularly interesting, especially chapters 2, 3 and 5.

There are however, numerous books on the social aspects of language (sociolinguistics) and Trudgill's first two or three chapters in *Sociolinguistics* are well expressed and provide a good introduction to this field.

Particularly worth recommending at this poi are three reference books which are dictionar of terms used in communication theory and linguistics. All the principal terms used in thi and other books are well explained and cross referenced. Especially useful to designers is tl *Dictionary of Communication and Media Studies* by Watson & Hill, as is *Key Concepts in Communication* from O'Sullivan, Hartley Saunders & Fiske. Both of these works have brief descriptions of a term and its concepts which provide excellent summaries of all the significant contributions to the theory and philosophy of communication. More speciali linguistic terminology can be found in Longman's *Dictionary of Applied Linguistic*

Defining the visible language

Linguists generally refer to the spoken language and the written language in order to differentiate between aural and visual forms of verbal communication. Their term 'writing system' covers writing and all mechanical forms of character generation and is very general. Writing is just one of several methods of visually recording the orthographic language; others include typing, printing and electronic generation of characters on a cathode ray tube. It is not the purpose here to delve into the technology involved, except in so far as the technology may have an effect upon the way in which the words are seen.

Hitherto, the term 'typography' has been used by printers and designers to cover the printed word in its various forms in much the same sense as the linguists' use of the general term writing system. Typography is arguably more pertinent as society deals far more with printed material than with material which has been handwritten. Since the advent of computers, filmsetters, dot-matrix and laser printers, the original definition of typography as 'the assembly of letters from movable metal type' is hardly accurate, but typography has survived in the professional world of the mass media and it now encompasses most of the new technology as a general term.

Visible language is a term which has found favour in recent years and more appropriately incorporates handwritten, drawn or mechanically constructed letters, all the orthographic forms, in fact, perceived by the eye. It is distinct from the term visual language because it is a system of arbitrary symbols which correspond to the smallest units of sounds in the spoken language, as opposed to more general images representing an expression of objects or concepts. Visible language and typography will be treated as synonymous and interchangeable terms throughout this book.

The orthographic or typographic system

The Western visible language is made up of a number of symbols (orthographic) which in the main represent sounds, plus some others (paragraphological) representing punctuation, mathematical signs, etc (Fig 26).

Fig 26

abcdefghijklmnopqrstuvwxyz
ABCDEFGHIJKLMNOPQRSTUVWXYZ
1234567890&,!?$(;^{1}/_

The letters of the alphabet (graphemes) usually correspond to a sound (phoneme) but there are a few logographs such as & and – which represent a whole word. Languages which have a spelling system which clearly indicates the pronunciation are called 'transparent' or 'regular'. Italian is an example which comes close to this. English is more complicated and certain combinations of letters sound the same as others, or the same combination may represent different sounds. George Bernard Shaw jokingly illustrated this by spelling the word 'fish' as 'ghoti', taking the 'gh' from 'enough', 'o' from women, and 'ti' from nation. Without delving into the full intricacies of the spelling system in English, the numerous irregularities in the language provide many problems for the learner but a rich vocabulary for the skilled reader – a feature which is constantly exploited by writers.

The system works by placing graphemes side by side to make up larger units of sound consisting of syllables and words. Each word is separated by a space and series of words are organised into phrases and sentences which are marked by punctuation. The letters of the alphabet, capitals and lower-case (the latter term derives from the early printers who placed the trays with the 'small' letters below the capital 'upper-case'), together with the punctuation marks, numerical symbols, etc, combine to form the system. Punctuation is vitally important and can change meaning quite dramatically (Fig 27).

A less dramatic illustration of the relationship of space between words (Fig 28) was a postcard which the author sent home to his teenage children while on holiday in Italy. Their initial response was astonishment at the sudden command of Italian which seemed very superior to the few words with which he had departed. It wasn't long, however, in trying to read it aloud, before they recognised that the 'message' was in fact the names of the Italian national football team, without capital letters and with the spaces between names re-arranged.

Fig 27

Missing comma sinks landmark

A PUNCTUATION error has led to the demolition of a listed Victorian British Rail waiting room.

The error came in a memo from a BR executive in London to BR in Scotland.

The memo listed all the rail facilities to be preserved. But in a sentence referring to Drem in East Lothian, it read "Drem Station bridge . . . ." should be retained.

This was taken by the railway engineers to mean that only the bridge was to be preserved and almost everything else was demolished.

After the waiting room was gutted and windows, lavatories and roof removed, the document was checked and it was realised that it should have read: retain "Drem Station, bridge . .".

The listed building was well known in the area and East Lothian District Council has insisted on its reconstruction and the reinstallation of 19th century fittings, including the cast iron drinking fountain.

Fig 28

Capital letters are used to mark the start of proper nouns and sentence beginnings. The Western language system is read from left to right and in lines from top to bottom. This seems a simple and logical system to Western eyes but it took a long time to evolve and other cultures developed systems in different ways – (Hebrew, for instance is read from right to left and the Chinese ideographic visible language system reads down the lines). It also requires some time to learn; children have to acquire the left to right movement of the eye along the line and to practise 'drawing' skills in repetitive left to right movements. The skilled reader, however, has absorbed the system and ceases to be conscious of it unless there is some deviation from the norm.

Most of the research into legibility and the pyschology of reading has been carried out using prose as 'continuous' text and the book as the norm. Comparatively little research has been undertaken on the visible language in the media and visual environment, which is from where most of the examples in this book are drawn. However, the conditions which constitute the norm in prose form are important in considering the effects on the visible language when those conditions are varied.

When graphemes are juxtaposed the letterforms make up a 'word shape' and the skilled reader sees word shapes, not just individual letters. The 'correct' juxtaposition of the letters is very important if the word shape is to be perceived in its familiar and recognisable form; letters must be arranged side by side, and reading from left to right. The word 'the' is so familiar it hardly needs to be seen, but if there is too much space between the letters as in:

t   h   e

or if the letters are placed in a vertical line underneath one another, the word shape is very different:

t
h
e

The practised reader has to note these individual shapes and reconstruct them mentally as a visual image in the correct order. The phrase 'a man of words and not of deeds' is quite difficult to read when it is set vertically (Fig 29). It is actually easier to read whole words turned on their side rather than split up the word shapes.

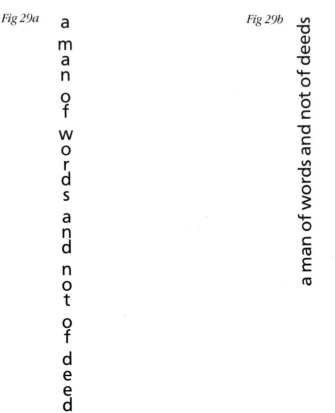

Fig 29a

Fig 29b

Considerable reasearch has been done since the last century on eye movement in reading, and this, along with other recent studies, is well set out in 'The Visible Word' (1968) by Herbert Spencer. In summary, the eye moves along a line of text in a series of rapid jerks (saccades) and pauses at a number of 'fixations' which takes in 10–12 letters (and spaces) at a time. It is surprising how close together the words can be in order for the space still to be noticeable in normal reading (Fig 30). Too much space between words is actually unhelpful for the eye to take in a reasonable number of characters, which can be as many as 30 characters in some cases. The eye seems to anticipate the left to right flow and takes in slightly more characters to the right of the fixation point. The average English word contains five characters plus one for the space and a normal line of text will contain around 60–70 characters, equivalent to ten to twelve words. It has been shown that lines of ten or twelve words allow the eye comfortably to make its series of 'saccades' before it sweeps back to make another series on the next and successive lines. Shorter lines may cause too many eye movements and become tiring if read in large quantities, and longer lines make it difficult on the return sweep to pick up the right line again, which means lines can be missed out.

It is important to remember that these 'optimum conditions' apply to adult reading book form. Approximately 2 mm high, the characters are usually 30–40 cm from the eye and are presented in large blocks of text, which involve the least 'interference' in this channel between the author and reader. The staccato movement of the eye along the line makes a number of regressions (returns to parts of the line previously scanned) during the process of reading, and deviations from the norm such too much space between words and too many words per line, can provoke more regressions and slow the reading process down.

Fig 30   The correct word space varies according to the design of the letterform but a useful guide isitheithicknessiofitheilower-caseii initheitypeisizeitoibeiused

During the last four or five hundred years of book production, many variations of the roman letterform have been created, but at the size and distance in the reading conditions set out above there is no significant difference between one design and another. Given good conditions, skilled readers will reach a reading rate of 300 words per minute. Faster reading speeds can be achieved but there is a limit to what can be comprehended. Most of the speeds claimed by faster reading techniques are greatly exaggerated. Skimming, or scanning lines rapidly to find key phrases of interest (which are then read normally for comprehension), is a reasonably safe way of coping with large amounts of text when time is at a premium.

Good reading conditions are not always present for all kinds of reasons. Compare 'visual interference' with listening to a speech which is not easy to hear if there are traffic noise, telephones ringing, or other people talking at the same time. There can be many forms of interference which make reception difficult. The Onneley implements sign (Fig 31) is an extraordinary example of visual 'noise' let in by mounting the letters onto a transparent grid so that perception is confused by the visual clutter in the background.

A cacophony of signs which form a large part of the visual environment (Fig 32 overleaf of pictures taken in Adelaide, Vienna, Milan and Tokyo) is taken for granted in our industrial society. It has been estimated by the advertising profession that in a modern city we are bombarded by 1,200 – 1,500 visual messages a day. Even where most of these are 'legible', too many can represent a lot of shouting of different messages at the same time!

Fig 31

Perception can also be confused by poor word formation. The sign 'CARAVAN NIGHT HALT' (Fig 33) has such a badly drawn 'G' that it looks like a 'C'. This sign was located on a road between Dover and London and as a result it is possible that visitors from Germany might interpret the sign as 'NICHT HALT', which is very close to the German phrase meaning the very opposite of what the sign intends to convey. Keeping to the visible norms can be very important. On the other hand, distortion may be taken to extremes and in an appropriate context still work effectively (Fig 34).

More commonly encountered (and less extreme) is a breaking of convention as in the sign 'please place your trays here' (Fig 35). The convention is that we read from left to right and to help this there should be more space between the lines than between the words. The spatial distribution within this sign would have us read 'please place trays your here'. The convention of left to right reading is much stronger than the optical relationship, but the spacing does not help the convention. Similarly, the 'Friarswood Playgroup' sign (Fig 36) is broken up arbitrarily by the constraints of the window. There is a good deal of tolerance on the part of the reader in this situation, who 'co-operates' by putting in the extra work required to decipher the words in their actual form. Many similar examples may be found which slow perception down unnecessarily.

Fig 33

Fig 34

The visible route to understanding

Most of the preceding section refers to the accuracy of perception in reading – the legibility of the visible language. The more difficult territory of 'understanding' – the cognitive aspects of reading – has justifiably received more attention in recent years.

Previously, it had been assumed that decoding the written or printed word and understanding the meaning of the symbols was dependent on the auditory system. When a word is spoken, the hearer identifies the sound from a known 'bank' of words and refers this to a semantic system to interpret the meaning. It was thought that reading a word set up a visual reference which was then converted into the auditory version before 'plugging-in' to the auditory word bank. Although this can happen, it is now accepted that skilled readers have a direct visual route to the semantic system in the brain. Research into computer recognition of the visible language and the evidence emanating from patients suffering from brain damage have supported this view.

ig 35

Fig 36

Children may use the auditory route when trying out a spelling to achieve correct pronunciation and in reading aloud. They are in reasonable command of the language by the time they are learning to read, but they are still extending their vocabulary in both the spoken and visible forms and building up both systems of recognition. For the skilled adult reader, there is little doubt that reading is faster than speaking (and speaking is faster than writing) and offers an independent although over-lapping means of access to a language facility in the brain.

This is expressed in a representation of the writing/reading/speaking relationship to the brain facility (Fig 37). It has been suggested that writing might be less efficient than speech for good communication, but that writing is better suited to the way the brain operates.

Fig 37

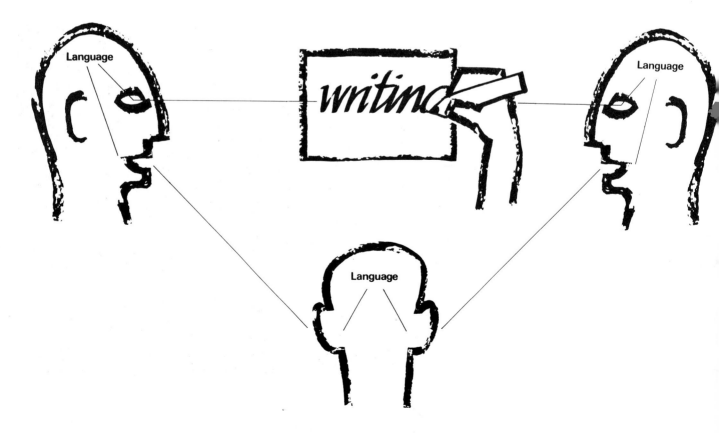

The visible language, we must conclude, does not simply express the spoken language visually. The letters do stand for sounds and in this sense the visible language is phonetic, but at another level it also shows similar looking words which are clearly related in meaning (morphemic) even though they sound different. The word 'euthanasia' is pronounced in virtually the same way as 'youth in asia' (see Fig 38). Conversely, there are many examples ('extreme', 'extremity') in which words are pronounced differently but have very close visual and semantic similarity.

Word recognition by either ear or eye route is an early stage of language communication; understanding the significance of words depends on the semantic system which links the meaning of the words (context) to the knowledge of the world (Fig 39). The 'Brighton Early' poster (Fig 40) relies upon the reader's knowledge of the phrase 'bright and early' to catch attention with the pun.

Fig 38

Fig 39

Grammar & Vocabulary

Linguistic Form

honology
ound)

Orthography
(visible signs)

Context
(relationship to world at large)

Interpretation

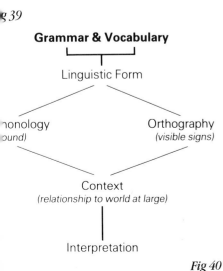

Fig 40

Changing the order of letters can alter the meaning of a word and changing the order of words can alter the meaning at a much wider level:

dog bites man

man bites dog

It would not be too surprising to see 'dog bites man' but 'man bites dog' would indicate extra-ordinary behaviour and enough to arouse curiosity as to the circumstances which led to this occurrence. We depend upon our knowledge of the world to sort out the complex ways in which words and structures are ordered to convey a variety of meanings. Reading is not simply a matter of interpreting the words which appear; the reader actively brings considerable knowledge (and personal bias) to bear on interpreting meaning. Whether the words are spoken or seen, there are numerous concepts which can be conveyed in comparatively short combinations:

'The old man threw a stick for the dog belonging to the Chairman's chauffeur.'

Concepts:
there is an old man
he throws a stick
there is a dog
the dog belongs to a chauffeur
the chauffeur is employed by the Chairman
(of a company)
etc . . .

Speech is often characterised by short bursts of information which are relatively independent, whereas writing is usually in slightly longer units which are more dependent upon one another. In the example sentence above, the second half is made a dependent clause by the subordinating conjunction 'belonging to' and is more typical of a written sentence than speech. There are at least five items of information in this 14 word sentence, which is basically one 'idea unit' of the old man (subject) (not 'any' man but an 'old' man) throwing a stick (verb) for the dog (object).

In speech, the number of ideas expressed in one utterance are usually quite brief and simple. It is thought that one idea in a clause of seven words is as much as our 'short-term memory' can handle. These phrases are expressed in about two seconds, have a coherent intonation and are preceded and followed by a pause. Each clause contains at least a verb and noun phrase as appropriate and although these conditions are not always present, they may be considered a norm for clear communication. Speech is composed spontaneously and can be further improvised on the spot to clarify or elaborate what has just been said. The act of writing is much slower mechanically but the writing can be re-composed and worked on in order to communicate clearly. It is read quickly, but can be re-read many times and ideas may be absorbed at the reader's individual pace. The visible language usually contains more information than does speech because ideas can be condensed in normally up to 11 words by the re-structuring which takes place in the writing. A good writer will not overdo this condensation and will maintain clarity by phrasing and judicious use of punctuation.

Differences between aural and visible languages

Clearly a visible language would not exist without the spoken word which provides the code system in sound form first. There are, however, important differences which have already been touched on. The historical precedents of printing as recording and reference 'tokens' in the form of lists and numbers are still apparent in the contemporary world. Despite the recording techniques for the voice and pictures in tapes, radio and television, the visible language – typography – is still the major alternative language form. Since the invention of radio and television, more books, magazines and printed matter have been produced than ever before. Titles and captions are necessary attributes for television, and computers present a large part of information in word form. The convenience of reading printed matter on paper, whether it is a book, brochure or letter, is a continuing facility requiring minimal technological aids.

The typographic language has been more stable than the spoken word due to the extra care and control which is taken over the production and the indefinite length of time that the recorded symbol survives in its written or printed form. Magazines and books are collected and stored for the value of the material contained within the covers, free of the context in which they were originally conceived and free of the 'face-to-face' personality of the author.

It would have been possible, before the advent of all the post-war media technology, to have clearly separated the special characteristics of the aural and visible language. Books, magazines, and other utilitarian forms and printing such as letterheads, forms, telephone directories, catalogues, etc, notices and other environmental signs, could have been listed on the one hand. On the other there would be the spoken word – informal, highly personalised, conversational dialogues which involve interaction of speakers and listeners. They could be shown theoretically as opposite ends of the language spectrum, but in practice there is so much borrowing of style which takes place between the two systems that it is difficult to divide them into 'compartments'. The spoken language tends to reveal its own processes of creation by its improvised nature, whereas the written form usually disguises the production processes and presents us with the polished and finished result. Radio and television broadcasts are often heavily scripted and have a similar information density to the written word. TV commercials are certainly very carefully contrived, whereas press and magazine advertising usually tries its best to imitate an informal conversational tone.

Reading continuous text

So far we have looked at the conditions for reading the visible language for perception and understanding. This has been based on simple word constructions and assembly of sentences into 'continuous text' in a familiar format such as that in which this book is printed. In this illustrated format the text is presented in fairly small, bite-size chunks, but as already shown, 10–12 words per line for a novel are more comfortable to read as far as eye movement is concerned. This division into lines bears little resemblance to the 'linear' character of speech which tries (at least) to make utterances in 'idea units' which are indicated by pauses between coherent units, or by just running out of breath. The ends of lines in book settings are somewhat arbitary and have been described as 'linear interrupted' (as opposed to the more standard term 'continuous'). However, as already indicated, access to 'language' can be either aural or visual and the settings of 10–12 words per line are as 'continuous' as may be achieved in the independent line of visual perception. That said, where the lines end, may be more crucial in other formats.

For example, children's books are almost always set out to follow the adult book format but in a large size of type. Little or no attention is paid to line endings or clauses which may be intended to be read together as idea units. This lack of consideration can hardly be a help to the learner. Fig 41 shows disregard even for word endings in the effort to square up the settings. It may be claimed that many children books are intended for parents to read to their children which is no doubt true up to a point but the visible language could be presented in a visual mode that is more appropriate for the inexperienced reader (Fig 42).

This is not an argument for the extension of the 'whole-sentence' method put forward in the 1870s. It is concerned more with a breaking down of the sentence into visible portions which relate more to the 'linear interruption' principle equivalent to speech.

There are many occasions when speech is required to be represented in a visual form which is more representative of the audio delivery. For example, linguists now have the facility to record word on tape (or video to include the paralinguistic signals) but, at some point or other, the discourse has to be transcribed onto paper for analysis or publication. Fig 43 overleaf is an experiment in transcribing a discourse between a headmaster and a pupil by using two different letterforms and a minimum of arbitrary linear interruptions.

Fig 42

When Owl was downstairs

he said, "I wonder

how my upstairs is?"

When Owl was upstairs

he said, "I wonder

how my downstairs

is doing?

I am always missing

one place or the other.

There must be a way," said Owl,

"to be upstairs

and to be downstairs

at the same time."

ig 41

ꓛETER was most dreadfully frightened; he rushed all ver the garden, for he had for-otten the way back to the gate. He lost one of his shoes mong the cabbages, and the ther shoe amongst the pota-oes.

Headmaster
Pupil

you know that i now **know** where you went don't you

we were in the woods

you went to stephen kennedys ho

i'm telling you the truth looking at me in the eyes and all that

ah no d d d don't interrupt me i warned you

i always find out

now i'm very displeased with you

because **you** set out to deceive me

quite delibera

and as i told you on friday that makes life very difficult

cos its means every time you and m you and i ta

so can i rely on that in future

yeah sorry about the whole thing

on't lie anna

we went to his house for a little while and then   he went meeting a girl

yes   **yes**

so all that messing about on friday

t in the end

i would know what happened

and perhaps you'll believe me when i tell you that next time

ah you asked me where

n   yeah h er n n n n

anna anna anna anna stop wriggling dear

you set out to deceive me

h other from now on

i'm going to have to think is that right **am i get** **d'you see**

d'you understand me

Prosodic visual cues

In speech, variations in pitch, loudness and speed are referred to as 'prosody'. In print different letter forms have been used to signify stress or emphasis since the end of the nineteenth century. The typesetting machines which dominated print production in the first half of this century contained a range of up to six or seven variations of the alphabet which were available in any one size:

ABCDEFGHIJKLMNOPQRSTUVWXYZ
abcdefghijklmnopqrstuvwxyz
£1234567890&.,:;!?(){}—
ABCDEFGHIJKLMNOPQRSTUVWXYZ
ABCDEFGHIJKLMNOPQRSTUVWXYZ
abcdefghijklmnopqrstuvwxyz
£1234567890&.,:;!?(){}—
ABCDEFGHIJKLMNOPQRSTUVWXYZ
abcdefghijklmnopqrstuvwxyz
£1234567890&.,:;!?(){}—

These were usually designed as a 'family set' consisting of capitals and lower-case in a roman style of normal weight, italic and bold versions of the roman, and sometimes a 'small capital' alphabet. These seven alphabets, together with the related numerals, punctuation marks and various signs and symbols, amounted to 272 characters which were easily set via a keyboard. The ready availability of these visual expressions of intonation, etc, have become conventions in the presentation of the visible language to a point where they are almost an essential part of the visual code system. However, this luxury of choice is not available to standard video text and computer VDU users where there are less than 100 characters, and there are considerable constraints on spatial distribution.

Paradoxically, at the same time as society is becoming more used to reading VDUs and dot matrix printouts, other comparatively cheap micro computers/word processors (desktop publishing) are now able to link up with very sophisticated filmsetters and laser printers, offering a tremendous range of letter styles.

The standard triad range of roman, italic and bold typefaces have been extremely useful in subtly but distinctly indicating different nuances in the language intended by the writ Used consistently, they represent different levels of discourse to be communicated between author and reader. In the face-to-fac discourse of the spoken word, speaker and hearer are able to interact spontaneously and both 'work' at making sense of what is being uttered.

The speaker watches for reactions in the hea and adopts different pragmatic strategies accordingly, and the hearer indicates understanding by nodding, grunting, etc, anc applying their own 'knowledge of the world in interpreting the implications in the speake choice of words. This kind of social communication is maintained by the willingness of the participants to co-operate actively and work hard together at their communicative attempts.

The opportunity for personal interaction is n normally available in writing/reading and all other forms of mass media communications. There is a 'distance' between the originator ai the receiver. There may be more than one reader/receiver at a time whether the form of communication is a poster, newsprint or cop of books spread across different continents, and the collective source of the authorship is often unknown. In addition to the structure and density of information in the compositio of the visible language, all the visual equivalents of the prosodic cues that can be mustered are invaluable aids to communica- tion. The small variations in weight or style c type may have little effect upon the legibility of the visible language, but they can have an important effect on the tone and attitudes which the author wishes to convey.

In reading continuous text, the flow of words from the author hold the attention and variations in style for emphasis, etc, are gentle aids to the general tone and sense. Conversely, as we shall see shortly, in large displays of visible language such as posters, advertisements and notices the style of letterform and layout are greatly exaggerated and have a conditioning effect upon the attitude of and interpretation made by the viewer.

Before leaving the world of 'small print' and moving into the display area which is the main concern, it is worth noting some other formats which are characteristic of the visual domain.

Alternative reading formats

Prose is the most common form in which we see visible language, but a close second is the list structure. Most lists could be strung together like prose, although they are seldom as easy to comprehend. A telephone directory is a list which is vertically structured so that the first letter of each entry can be scanned downwards, and would be unimaginable as prose (Fig 44). Information set out in tabular form is read across and down and can be in words or any combinations of words and mathematical signs (Fig 45). Such structures are as old as writing itself and are conventions now being transferred to videotext. The railway timetable incorporates abbreviations which are explained in footnotes, and also a few other visual signs representing buffet car or restaurant facilities, etc. These kinds of signs, symbols and other forms of visual communication are outside the scope of this book which is concerned only with the alphanumeric/typographic signs which form the visible language system.

Fig 44

324-7250	**Paine Robert**	
	Between The Lakes Rd Slsbry	
324-0569	**Pajarola B** Sunrise Ridge Slsbry	
324-0017	**Pallone Pasquale J** Bragg N Cnan	
324-0237	**Palmer Dale D** 271 Dublin Rd	
324-7328	**Palmer Frederick**	
	S Canaan Rd Fls Vlg	
324-5882	**Palmer Jeffrey J** 268-A Dublin Rd	
324-7501	**Palmer Martin F**	
	Music Mountain Rd Fls Vlg	
324-0342	**Palmer Mary Dale** Dublin Rd Fls Vlg	
324-0364	**Palmer Richard M** Route 126	
324-0897	**Palmer S** Prospect-N Cnan	
324-0871	**Palmer William C** Miner	
324-7176	**Palmieri Gary** Route 126 Fls Vlg	
324-5937	**Paramount Laundromat**	
	Church-N Cnan	
324-0842	**Pardon Roger E** Twin Lakes Rd Slsbry	
324-7832	**Parker Hugh T**	
	Housatonic River Rd Slsbry	
324-0483	**Parker Kenneth** Weatogue Rd Slsbry	
324-5259	**Parker Leo W** Birch La N Cnan	
324-5426	**PARKSIDE LODGE OF**	
	CONNECTICUT Route 7	
324-5950	**Parmlee Floyd** Barlow	
324-0501	**Parsons Carl**	
	Music Mountain Rd Fls Vlg	
324-5926	**Parsons Donald**	
	Music Mountain Rd Fls Vlg	
324-7720	**Parsons Donald Jr**	
	Music Mountain Rd	
324-7992	**Parsons Everice** College Hill	
324-5003	**Paruta John** East Canaan	
324-0232	**Pasqualina Robert & Janet**	
	Beebe Hill Rd	
324-7882	**Passini Alfred** South Canaan	
324-7626	**Pastori Martin** N Canaan Rd	
324-0543	**Patchen Elester** Raymond Av N Cnan	
324-5011	**Patterson L**	
	Granite Avenue Ext-N Cnan	
324-7000	**Patterson Leroy A**	
	Under Mountain Rd Fls Vlg	
324-0113	**Patterson Robert**	
	Between The Lakes Rd	
324-0068	**Patterson Robert I**	
	Under Mountain Rd Fls Vlg	
324-5716	**Pautot Robert J** Raymond Av N Cnan	
324-5661	**Paviol Martin** Brown's La N Cnan	
324-7234	**Paviol Raymond** East Canaan	
324-7036	**Paviol Thomas E** East Canaan	

Fig 45

WESTBOUND — TO BROOKLYN — Effective May 22, 1989

MONDAY TO FRIDAY, EXCEPT HOLIDAYS

Leave			Arrive	Leave			Arrive	Leave			Arrive	Leave			Arrive	Leave			Arrive
Ja-maica	East-New York	Nos-trand Ave.	Flat-bush Ave.	Ja-maica	East New York	Nos-trand Ave.	Flat-bush Ave.	Ja-maica	East New York	Nos-trand Ave.	Flat-bush Ave.	Ja-maica	East New York	Nos-trand Ave.	Flat-bush Ave.	Ja-maica	East New York	Nos-trand Ave.	Flat-bush Ave.
AM	AM	AM	AM	AM	AM	AM	AM	AM	AM	AM	AM	PM	PM	PM	PM	AM	AM	AM	AM
■12 06	....	....	12 22	7 46	7 54	7 59	8 04	11 16	11 24	11 29	11 34	5 33	....	5 45	5 50	T12 06	....	....	12 22
M12 14	....	....	12 30	7 53	....	....	8 09	11 33	....	....	11 49	5 48	....	6 00	6 05	T12 14	12 21	12 26	12 31
■12 14	12 21	12 26	12 31	7 56	....	....	8 12	11 44	11 51	11 55	12 00	5 54	6 02	6 07	6 12	Y12 14	....	....	12 30
M12 17	12 25	12 30	12 35	7 59	8 07	8 12	8 17	12 07	12 14	12 19	12 24	6 13	....	....	6 29	Y12 17	12 25	12 30	12 35
12 33	....	....	12 51	8 06	....	....	8 22	12 25	....	12 37	12 42	6 40	6 48	6 53	6 58	12 33	....	....	12 51
12 43	12 51	12 56	1 01	8 09	....	....	8 25	12 33	....	....	12 48	7 01	....	7 13	7 18	12 43	12 51	12 56	1 01
1 15	1 23	1 28	1 33	8 16	8 24	....	8 33	12 54	....	....	1 10	7 07	7 15	7 20	7 25	1 15	1 23	1 28	1 33
1 47	1 55	2 00	2 05	8 23	....	....	8 36	1 07	1 14	1 19	1 24	7 33	....	7 45	7 50	1 47	1 55	2 00	2 05
2 05	....	....	2 21	8 26	....	8 40	8 45	1 33	....	....	1 49	7 40	7 48	....	7 57	2 19	2 27	2 32	2 37
2 15	2 23	2 28	2 33	8 33	8 41	8 46	8 51	1 45	1 52	1 56	2 01	8 01	....	8 13	8 18	2 44	2 52	2 57	3 02
2 33	2 41	....	2 50	8 44	8 51	8 56	9 01	2 07	....	2 19	2 24	8 09	8 17	8 22	8 27	4 30	4 37	4 42	4 48
3 50	....	....	4 06	8 52	....	....	9 08	2 20	2 28	2 33	2 38	8 33	....	....	8 49	4 43	4 51	4 56	5 01
4 35	4 43	4 48	4 53	8 58	9 06	9 11	9 16	2 33	....	....	2 49	8 46	8 54	8 59	9 04	5 43	5 51	5 56	6 01
5 33	5 41	5 46	5 51	9 05	....	....	9 21	3 07	3 14	....	3 23	9 06	....	9 18	9 23	6 13	6 21	6 26	6 31
5 54	6 02	6 07	6 12	9 14	....	....	9 30	3 16	3 24	3 29	3 34	9 26	9 34	....	9 43	6 43	6 51	6 56	7 01
6 13	6 21	6 26	6 32	9 17	9 25	9 30	9 35	3 33	....	....	3 49	9 33	....	....	9 49	AM	AM	AM	AM
6 35	6 44	6 49	6 54	9 34	9 42	9 46	9 51	3 43	3 51	3 56	4 01	10 00	....	....	10 16				
6 50	6 58	7 03	7 08	9 45	....	....	10 01	4 07	4 15	4 20	4 25	10 09	10 16	10 21	10 26				
7 04	7 12	7 17	7 22	10 00	....	....	10 19	4 24	4 31	4 36	4 42	10 33	....	....	10 50				
7 11	....	....	7 27	10 07	10 14	10 19	10 24	4 41	....	4 53	4 58	10 46	10 53	....	11 02				
7 14	7 22	....	7 31	10 29	....	....	10 45	4 57	....	....	5 13	11 06	....	11 18	11 23				
7 24	7 32	7 37	7 41	10 33	10 40	10 45	10 50	5 09	5 17	5 22	5 27	11 33	....	....	11 50				
7 32	7 40	7 45	7 50	11 07	....	....	11 23	....	....	....	....	....	....	....	....				
7 41	....	....	7 58	....	....	....	....	....	....	....	....	....	....	....	....				
7 43	7 51	7 56	8 01	....	....	....	....	....	....	....	....	....	....	....	....				
AM	AM	AM	AM	AM	AM	AM	AM	PM	PM	PM	PM	PM	PM	PM	PM				

'Display' text, to use the conventional typographic term, covers the design arrangement of headlines, slogans, titles, advertisements, etc. This includes the choice of letterforms, how the words are arranged in relation to one another, and their relationship to the space in which they are inserted. Poetry falls somewhere between continuous text and display text, in that it is deliberately arranged to comply with poetic conventions. The student exercise (Fig 46) show how these stages can sometimes stretch as far as a visual portrayal of the poem's subject matter.

Twentieth-century poetry in particular has been subject to special typographic treatmer and in some cases the results have entered th domain of abstract art. Display text, howeve usually applies to the larger visual sizes of letterforms used in publicity and the news media, on notices and other environmental signs.

Fig 46

THE MASTER

That face.
That face like a lump of suet
moulded,
kneeded.
That unmistakable face
That face that launched a thousand,
screams,
gasps,
bitten finger nails.
That face.
Like an overgrown cocker spaniel
wanting to be fed.
And that body,
bulky,
fleshy,
soft,
like that face.
With those lips,
pouting,
puffing,
protruding,
echoing the paunch.
With the hands hugging,
fingers clasping,
thumbs touching,
In the famous stance,
that matches the profile,
that goes with,
That face.

THE MASTER

That face.
That face like a lump of suet
moulded,
kneeded.
That unmistakable face
That face that launched a thousand,
screams,
gasps,
bitten finger nails.
That face.
Like an overgrown cocker spaniel
wanting to be fed.
And that body,
bulky,
fleshy,
soft,
like that face.
With those lips,
pouting,
puffing,
protruding,
echoing the paunch.
With the hands hugging,
fingers clasping,
thumbs touching,
In the famous stance,
that matches the profile,
that goes with,
That face.

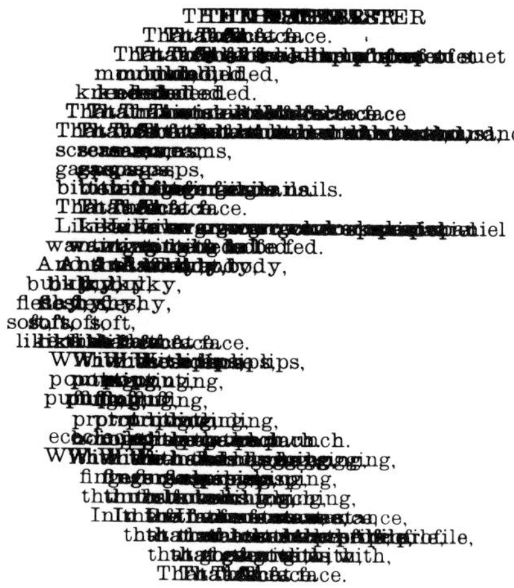

Another common use of the alphanumeric visual code is for utilitarian purposes such as forms, notepaper, etc, which are intended to be written (or typed) on. In a sense, these are 'question and answer' discourses conducted at a distance, primarily for bureaucratic purposes (Fig 47). Letterheadings ostensibly have the name and address of the sender printed on them in order to save time in writing or typing out the information each time, but the prestige value of printed notepaper also has a value for publicity purposes.

An interesting variant is the flow chart or logical tree structure which has been used in recent years for instructional or form-filling purposes. Instead of using prose in continuous text, statements or questions can be ordered in a simple sequence requiring a 'yes/no' or 'either/or' answer. This can be presented as a list or in diagrammatic format (Fig 48). The advantage of this hierarchical structure is that only those parts of the prose that are relevant to each situation need to be read and answered, instead of having to wade through all the alternatives contained in the continuous text version.

Fig 47

Fig 48

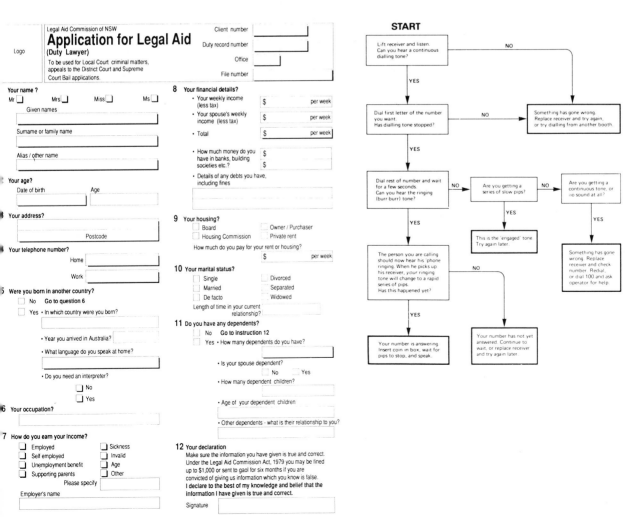

Categorising the various modes in which the visible language system is used is a daunting task, and as yet there is no consensus from the various attempts which have been made. The categories may be constantly refuted and re-defined in opening this particular Pandora's box, and so a fairly simple diagram is offered (Fig 49) which is inevitably inconclusive, but may help to identify the general areas outlined in the above.

It is clear that a great deal of work has been undertaken in both the aural and visible fields of language by psychologists, linguists and social scientists. In the latter half of this century, linguists have explored the spoken word under many headings and their attention to the so-called 'written' language has concentrated on prose as continuous text in literature and the media. The legibility of machine-made characters has been examined extensively, and some research has been carried out on 'pure information' communication in the utilitarian field of forms and tables, etc, notably at the Medical Research Council Applied Psychology Unit, Cambridge, and the Communication Research Institute of Australia, etc.

In addition, the comparatively new area of 'Communication Studies' which includes semiotic (ie relating to signs and symbols and their meanings) as well as linguistic analysis, has begun to draw the separate disciplines together in an attempt to provide a comprehensive theoretical basis for analysis.

Among this very broad range of language forms, the area loosely defined under 'Display' has received limited linguistic attention. When it has occurred in linguistics it has been mainly concerned with advertising and political propaganda and has been analysed as if it were part of continuous text, with little regard for size, style and layout which are essential features of presentation in the media. At least much thought and effort is applied to contriving this presentation in assembling the right words. The manipulation of language in the public domain, to influence the thoughts and actions of social groups, is acknowledged as an important aspect of language awareness. The manipulation of the visible language as a visual 'tone of voice' needs to be taken into account.

Fig 49

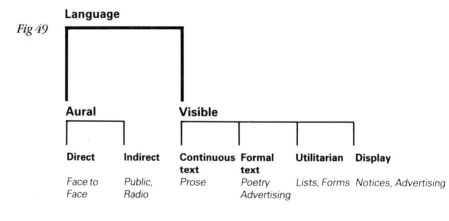

The Visible Word by Herbert Spencer, although over 20 years old now, is probably the best summary of the research into the legibility of typeface design. Many other books on typography contain a chapter or so on legibility, but few are as comprehensive or as objective as Spencer's survey, which contains references to all the major research carried out this century.

A more recent publication for the Open University (UK) is Ellis' *Reading, Writing & Dyslexia*. This also has an excellent opening chapter on the origins of writing, but it is chapters 2 and 3 which encapsulate the differences between decoding the aural and the visible language systems. Readers can work out for themselves what else they might wish to devour as each chapter concludes with a summary.

Another excellent book on the cognitive understanding of the visible language is *The Psychology of Reading* by Robert Crowder of Yale University. This is a very thorough examination of the same ground, well illustrated and again, easily selected for chapter readings via a summary at the end of each chapter.

More linguistically orientated, *Language and Literacy* (Stubbs), again contains many pertinent observations which are relevant to this subject area, and designers as well as linguists should study this important book.

Content, form, context

Content and *form* are essential elements in making a message. A similar distinction has been made between a 'digital' code (in this case, words) and an 'analogic' code which expresses and elicits feelings about the message (paralinguistic, iconic). Placed in an appropriate *context* as the important third element, communication can take place. In the spoken language, the content is the phonology, syntax and semantic structure of the words (sound, sequence and meaning). The form is the prosodic delivery of the words, that is the rate, accent, intonation, range, etc. Prosody has been described as 'a kind of musical accompaniment to speech'. The command 'give it to me' could have the stress on 'give', 'it', or 'me' and the emphasis is changed each time. It could be uttered by a child in a whining tone and, given a particular context, might be recognised as a request rather than a command. Given another context, it could be an offer of help.

Written language and typography have parallel levels of content, form and context. The content is the spelling, syntax and semantic structure of the words and the form is the visual nature and arrangement of the typography. In addition there are the prosodic cues of stress or intonation, and the spoken word is usually accompanied by facial expressions, eye movements and gestures as paralinguistic signs (unless one is listening to radio, for instance). The style of the letterforms, size, weight and spatial distribution are the visual counterparts to the prosodic cues and paralinguistics. Just two letters – the word 'me' – can connote different interpretations by entirely visual means (Figs 50, 51, 52). The introverted whisper in Fig 50 is contrasted by the bold, 'shout' version in Fig 51. There is an informal and more personalised version expressed in Fig 52. These impressions are the result of shape, size and space. We shall look at those aspects in turn.

Fig 50   *Fig 51*   *Fig 52*

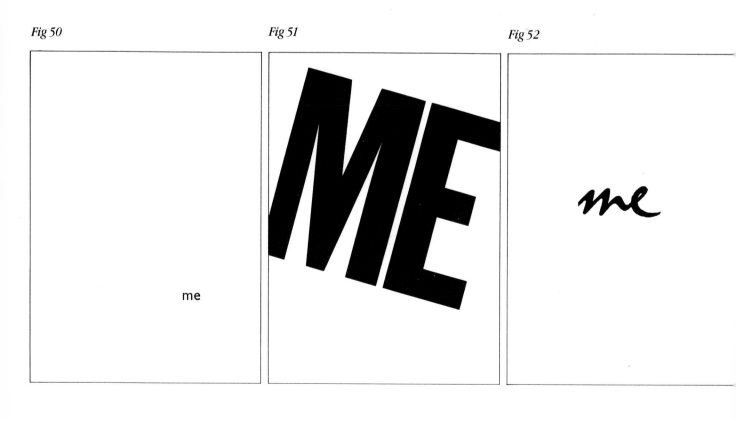

Shape (Letterforms)

The connotations which are stimulated by particular letterforms are historical and social. They are interpreted by our 'knowledge of the world' and are part of the cultural context of society. The western alphabet evolved from the Phoenicians via the Greek and Roman civilizations. It was the latter which gave the visual form to our 'roman' alphabet, and the inscribed capital letters of 2,000 years ago still provides the basic proportions for what we consider to be aesthetically pleasing. In the same historical sense, the handwritten minuscules of around the tenth century provide the model upon which our lower case alphabet is based. The number of variations in the design of the roman alphabet since the invention of printing have been quite incredible considering the constraints of the basic structure. Despite the thousands of variations, virtually all may be grouped into four basic types (Fig 53), which have become known as 'Old Face' (also Garalde) 'Modern Face' (also Didone), Sans Serif and lastly Egyptian (also Slab Serif).

Usually (but not always), the cultural association which a reader has from any of these letter styles is rooted in their historical origin. It is easy to select typeface designs which have developed in a particular national culture and which now connote the 'ish-ness' of that country (Fig 54). For example, one of the most famous handwritten books is the *Book of Kells* produced in Ireland 1,200 years ago, which still provides the style for the stereotype design (Fig 54e) which is used many times over to denote an Irish ethnic connection. Few readers would know this origin, but the repeated use reinforces and perpetuates the stereotype.

Fig 53

d Old Face

d Modern

d Sans Serif

d Egyptian

Fig 54a–e

English

American

German

Italian

írísh

Emil Ruder makes this point in relation to continuous text typefaces:

'... the various cultural centres of Europe began to grow apart and to print in their own national languages, using their various national typefaces. The development of national typefaces is closely bound up with the differences between national languages. Garamond is intimately associated with the French language, Caslon with the English, Bodoni with the Italian. If one of these is used for a foreign language, it may forfeit a great deal of its effect'.

Ruder later points out that some designs in more recent times have very little 'national' character and may be used in a variety of languages – the standard typewriter letterform being one of the earliest examples of an 'International' typeface design.

In the period from 1500–1800, it is understandable that difficulties in communication across frontiers would have aided the development of separate national characteristics, especially as printing was established throughout Europe by then and had a stabilising effect upon the fluctuations of language and style within the national borders. Such a period of time, with all its visual manifestations, becomes part of a cultural heritage and is then deeply embedded in it. (Ruder's book on typography had a similar effect on style, albeit for a shorter period, in that it encapsulated the visual paradigm of the 1960s and dominated the 'International Style' of that and the next decade).

Fig 55

Fig 56

Fig 57

The taken-for-granted visual style (Figs 55, 56) is a mixture of the long-held, deeply entrenched knowledge of the culture in which we grow up, with all its fashionable trends and current fads incorporated in a dynamic, fluctuating flow of the living language. What was a fashionable style of its period when first used in Paris (Fig 57) is now an evocative image which is part of the Parisian street scene. A different kind of connotation is evoked by the shop sign 'coiffure' (Fig 58), partly out of the cultural association of hairstyling with Paris, and the French word (to an English/American speaking community), but primarily from the visual similarity of the letters to curves of hair. This, like the North Wales shop sign (Fig 59) where the letters are joined together like a string of wool, enters the iconic world and almost becomes an ideogram, where the word and the meaning become one image. An example of the power of the visual character is the Israeli tee-shirt (Fig 60) which shows a well-known name in an unfamiliar language and an even more unfamiliar Hebrew alphabet, but which is still instantly recognisable as 'Coca-Cola'.

Connotation

The traditional virtues of strength, dignity, warmth, etc, have been shown to be associated with certain typestyles and abstract tests of typestyles and their connotations have been carried out since the 1920s. Connotations in German or Italian would not necessarily translate into English as connotations are clearly culture-specific. In almost all research, the varieties of letterforms have been investigated by testing styles of alphabets against associations with emotive words. In order to avoid words in a context of sentences which would condition the semantic interpretation placed on them, alphabets of typestyles or isolated words have been used in the traditional format for this research. What would be interesting would be to approach the evaluation from the opposite end to discover the extent to which meaning may be affected by style (as in Figs 50, 51, 52). Professional designers use intuition in making these layout decisions, and although research has shown that this intuition is reasonably accurate in accommodating public interpretation, it may not always be the case.

Fig 58

Fig 60

Fig 59

The connotative qualities of drawn letterforms are well known, and the amount of unskilled examples which are frequent sights in our environment establish their own visual register. The 'Teas and Home Made Cakes' sign (Fig 61) is typical of its genre and by its uneven, 'non-machine-made' letterforms tells the reader that everything is indeed home-made and establishes its credibility. Less convincing would be a polished, professional sign that clearly is not the hand that makes the tea and cakes. This can be seen in reverse as it were, by looking at the hand-painted sign on the local builder's van (Fig 62) and the dentist's nameplate (Fig 63). As they exist, they are entirely appropriate for the context of the 'service offered' to the client. If these styles were to be transposed it would be difficult for the dentist to inspire the expected confidence in his ability! In comparison, it is clear that the same hand-painted 'fish for sale' and 'art exhibition' signs, making a surprising connection between them (Fig 64).

It is usually accepted that the emotive connotations of letterforms are more applicable to printed communications which are intended to 'persuade' as opposed to those which simply offer 'information'. The latter is expected to be presented in a neutral typestyle of 'maximum clarity'. It is significant therefore of the accepted associations that a less legible letterform (to English readers), the so-called Gothic or Old English style (Fig 65), was recommended as recently as 1970 by the HMSO publication *Design of Forms* – 'The use of special type for legal or solemn effect may be desirable for some declarations'. The 'Gothic' or 'Old English' letterform has a strong connotation of antiquity and, in addition to its legalistic use, it is the most frequent typestyle used by antique dealers. It also survived well into the twentieth century in Germany as the standard letter form in common use, hence an association with Germanic texts (see Fig 54c).

Fig 61   *Fig 62*   *Fig 63*

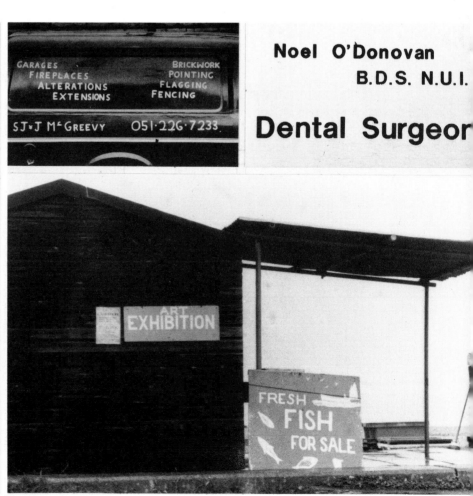

Fig 64

Letterforms based on 'copperplate' handwriting of the eighteenth and nineteenth centuries similarly have a connotation of antiquity and are also favoured by old established institutions such as those in the legal profession. These conventions are subject to changes as the social climate changes and it is sometimes quite complex for a modern legal practice to demonstrate that it can speak in the language of today, and still show it has the traditional virtues of long legal experience (Fig 66). In a distinct contrast to the very conservative British expectation, it is not unusual for Danish solicitors to have quite modern and even abstract designs for their notepaper (Fig 67).

There is no equivalent terminology in the aural language to 'readability', but the pleasure derived from listening to a good speaker in the after-dinner speech, a brilliant lecture, or the inspiring rhetoric of a politician, is supplied by a combination of the creative exploitation of linguistic features and metaphorical structures, with a flowing articulate delivery, usually well-prepared and rehearsed. It is the latter capacity of well-prepared writing which enables the creative aspects to be exploited to their best advantage in the visible language. In prose (continuous text), the reader may enjoy a well-structured order of words which an author has worked out, with minimum interference from the layout. In display texts, there is an additional feature of the visual structure to appeal to the aesthetic sensitivity of the reader.

ig 65

Fig 66

Fig 67

Aesthetics

A sense of beauty as a visual phenomena is
inherent in humans and has been a characteristic
of mark-making long before the advent of any
writing system. Whatever the tool used, scribes
have endeavoured to make letterforms of
clarity and beauty. The designs of typefaces
have considered the same problems of
proportion and shape (based upon those of
the Roman era). It is mainly the limitations of
current computing technology which have
produced the crude alphanumerics on so many
VDUs and printouts, hopefully a temporary
phase. The presence (or absence) of aesthetic
form in all other genres of the visible language,
can have a reconciling influence (or jarring in
its absence!) on the acceptability of the message.

Taken to extremes, the passion for beauty can
exceed any consideration for legibility and
become an exercise in calligraphic impression-
ism (Fig 68), or as has been commented: 'we
are blessed with . . . a language the writing of
which in the most informal circumstances is
susceptible to style and beauty'.

Fig 68

Size and Space

The normal reading size is understood to be the size used in books in setting continuous text (between 8pt and 14pt). Words set in larger sizes are generally expected to have more emphasis, or are more important, and signify titles, or headings and subheads. Books, magazines and newspapers are read within an arm's length (Fig 69) and may contain very large letters which are intended to gain attention as much as provide headings. The external environment provides an even wider range of sizes, tempered by the perspective and distance.

An exception to the 'large means pay attention' rule is the larger sizes generally found in children's books or early reading texts. Traditional theory assumes that a larger size enables the learner to more easily discern the individual letter shapes. At what point the child adopts the norm may be debatable, and tests carried out in the 1960s led to the conclusion that 'the smaller the child, the smaller the type'. In more recent research projects on large type sizes, which examined advertisements set in 18pt and/or larger, no significant difference in 'readability' was found. Size *in itself*, seems to have little influence on legibility or readability.

Fig 69

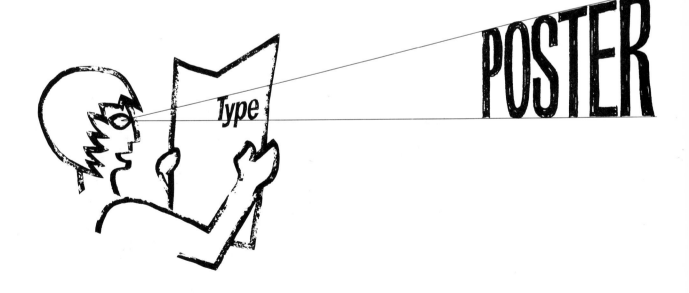

More pertinent to display is the *scale* of letters in relation to the surface area and any other images which may be encompassed within the same area. Environmental graphics are seldom controlled to the extent where the surroundings are taken into account in a total design solution (an exception to this is the siting of motorway signs). Despite some attempts by local authorities to exercise control, the scale of signs on buildings is in effect arbitrary and anarchic, whereas printed communications are usually planned to a greater or lesser degree, to conform within a standard range of paper sizes.

Words printed within a rectangular area, for example, can be set in a sliding scale of sizes which might generally correspond to whispering, quiet, normal, loud speaking, ar shouting (Fig 70, 71), particularly if the weig ratio (thickness of letters) increases proportionately. Seen within the border of tl frame, the word/s may appear more importar or 'louder'. The frame provides the visual context for 'scale' to be meaningful. It is difficult to extract the purely visual factors from the semantic dimension of the words, k it is clear that although size may be immateri to legibility, it can be significant in the interpretation.

Fig 70

Fig 71

G'DAY!

G'DAY!

The use of different sizes within one frame normally indicates a hierarchy of importance. It may indicate by size, rather than starting at the left-to-right, head-to-foot sequencing, what should be seen/read first (Fig 72). An unusual example of a contrast of size being used to 'foreground' words (Fig 73) contrives to pull out keywords contained in the linear text and these are read first as a 'telegraphed' abbreviated message. This kind of foregrounding can be achieved visually in other ways – colour for example. The spatial distribution is also of crucial importance in the interpretation of the visible language in addition to perceptual problems outlined earlier.

Foregrounding by size is a very obvious strategy often used in visual presentation and is fundamental to the hierarchy of reading order and importance. It is unfortunate that this is frequently ignored by linguists when analysing text which is 'displayed' and not in continuous prose form. An analysis of language in displayed visual form must include the basic visual strategies of presentation.

Fig 72

Your new **hot line** to Carl Reilly Jnr is 824-5744 East Canaan

Fig 73

Form versus function

Aesthetic considerations have always played a
prominent role in giving the language visible
form. The traditional convention of visually
balancing lines of text around a central vertical
axis (symmetrical) is no less dictatorial towards
the shape of the language than its twentieth-
century paradigm of 'off-centred', 'range left'
asymmetrical style. Jan Tschichold claimed that
'in central typography, pure form comes before
the meaning of the words'.

The sixteenth century example (Fig 74) show
line endings which have total disregard for th
words in order to produce a visually attractiv
arrangement. It is paralleled by the cover des
by Swiss designer Hans Lutz (Fig 75) which
ignores the left to right 'legible' word shape
convention, to make a visual pattern which
reads down. As a booklet on typography,
taking liberties with the conventions is
perfectly appropriate.

Fig 74

INTSITV
TIO PRINCIPIS CHRI
ftiani, faluberrimis refer
ta præceptis. p Eraſ
mum Roteroda-
mum, ab eo,
dem reco,
gnita
cũ alijs nó,
nullis eôdé ptiné
tibus, quorũ catalogũ
in ,pxima reperies pagella.
APVD INCLYTAM
BASILEAM.

Fig 75

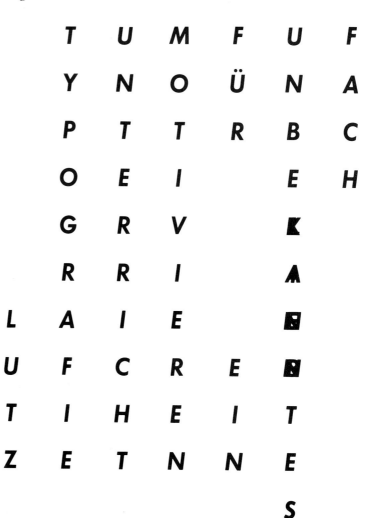

Each era produces its own visual style according to the cultural values of the society of that period. The practice of arranging words in square boxes at the expense of different letter and word spacing (Figs 76, 77) has been an aesthetic device, on-and-off, over hundreds of years and enjoyed another vogue in the 1980s.

The idea of squaring-up the letters into rectangular shapes may have been prompted by the mechanics of the metal typesetting process where it is easy and fairly natural to spread the letters across each line, but it is more likely that it is an aesthetic device to 'balance' the block of words and fit the rectangular page. Computer technology now makes it even easier to distort and bend the letter forms to fit almost any shape.

g 76

Fig 77

ELECTRIC
FURNACES

ROYCE & BROWNE 6 GRAFTON MEWS, LONDON, W.1

TELEPHONE:
MUSEUM 0345
TELEGRAMS:
BROYCELECT
EUSROAD, LONDON
CABLEGRAMS:
BROYCELECT LONDON

ELECTRIC FURNACES FOR ALL USES INCLUDING ENAMELLING, STAINED GLASS, LABORATORIES, TILEMAKING, POTTERY

FOR ALL INDUSTRIAL AND SCIENTIFIC PURPOSES, ETC.

Deliberate flaunting of reading conventions in creating textual visual patterns may be due to rebellion against such conventions (Fig 78), or a combination of visual appeal together with foregrounding of keywords within the text (Fig 79 opposite). Such variables may be temporary and subject to fashion changes and influences from other visual fields, but they can be imposed on the visible language and inevitably affect the semantic interpretation in much the same way as a regional accent or 'solemn tone' can affect the aural language.

It is important that the various factors outline[d] in this section are recognised and taken into account by the eye. 'Literacy' in terms of pub[lic] communications is both linguistic and visual.

Fig 78

SIGHT   SOUND

[marginal references, SIGHT: 10,000 Maniacs: on 19; George Steiner: in 6 p.17; George Steiner: in 6 p.33; George Steiner: in 6 p.45; Eric Gill: in 20 p.52; George Steiner: in 6 p.31 0; Ivan Illic h in 21 p.125]

SIGHT — 'any modern man can see, SCIENCE, is TRUTH FOR LIFE, watch RELIGION fall obsolete, SCIENCE, will be TRUTH FOR LIFE, TECHNOLOGY AS NATURE, SCIENCE, TRUTH FOR LIFE, IN FORTRAN TONGUE THE ANSWER.'

'A philosophy of language would return with radical wonder to the fact that language is the defining mystery of man, that in it, his identity and historical presence are uniquely explicit. It is language that severs man from the deterministic signal codes, from the silences that inhabit the great er part of our being. If silence were again to come to a ruined civilisation, it would be a two-fold silence, desperate with the remembrance of the word.'

ntury that significant areas of truth, reality and action reced e from the sphere of verbal st atement. Between these langu ages (algebra, architecture) an d that of common usage, between the mathe matical symbol and the w ord, the bridges grow mor e and more tenuous, until at last they are down...Th is is a fact of tremendous im plication. It has divided the experience and perceptio n of reality into separate d omains.'

'THE INSTRU MENT IN OU R HANDS IS WORN BY L ONG USAGE, And the deman ds of mass cultu re and mass co

'We shall shortly have a s ituation wherein all jokes & eccentricities are the w ork of DESIGNERS- & ma chine-made jokes reprod uced by the million TEND TO BE BORING' 'IT BECOMES EASIER &

'The style of p olitics and FA CTUAL com munication ve rges on the illi terate. Whethe r in its adverti sements, its co mic books, or its television, our culture liv es by the pictu

SOUND — 'The primacy of the wor d carried over into Ch ristianity the belief that all truth and realness, with th e exception of a small queer margin at the very top, can b e housed within the walls of language. It is during the seventeenth ce

'The style is a mosaic. Each word is set up in its precise and luminou s place. Touc h by touch, Durrell builds his array of sensuous, rare expr essions into patterns of ima gery and tactile suggestion so subtle and convoluted tha t the act of reading becomes one of total sensual appreh ension. Paragraphs live to th e touch of the reader's hand; they have a complex aural m usic; and the light seems to p lay across the surface of the words in bright tracery. No one else writing in English to day has quite the same com mitment to the light and mu sic of language.'

'Only he who discovers the help of writ ten words in   '...in choosi ng his text, th e artist cho oses words

[marginal references, SOUND: George Steiner in 6; George Steiner in 6 9; Nicol e Gra n 1 p]

BULLETIN

■■ A double, and deadly, dose of **Rutger Hauer** at the cinema in May. This is not a public health warning: Hauer is the Dutch heavy who played the blond android in Blade Runner, and lends his considerable screen presence to *two* of May's recommended films, **The Hitcher** and **Flesh And Blood**.

Strictly speaking, it is now Six Years With THE FACE (no cards, no [fl]owers, no fuss please) but [th]e Photographers Gallery [t]ouring exhibition FIVE [Y]EARS WITH THE FACE [k]eeps rolling along. See it [at] the Mostyn Art Gallery in [Ll]andudno from April 19-[M]ay 18 and in Sheffield [th]roughout June.

Reviews p105 ■■ Acerbic, obsessive and coruscatingly funny, one-time FACE columnist **Ray Lowry** has few rivals as a single-frame cartoonist. **This Space To Let** (Abacus, £2.95) is the paperback version ■■ **No Pay No Way** is the title of a seven-minute scratch video from **Death Valley Days** with the provocative message rap: "Eat the rich, not junk food". Burger polemics available from **Guerilla Tapes** 01-609 8536 ■■ **Pravda**, David Hare and Howard Brenton's 'comedy of the year' about the Street Of Shame, sold out every performance on its first run. It starts a welcome new season at the National Theatre from May 2 with **Anthony Hopkins** returning as the predatory press baron Lambert Le Roux ■■ Similar ground is covered in Australian David Williamson's play **Sons Of Cain** — at London's Wyndhams Theatre from May 16. Power and corruption in the press, Australian version, from the writer who scripted Gallipoli and The Year Of Living Dangerously ■■ Record of the month: **Janet Jackson**'s "Control" LP (A&M) is another sparkler from the pop-soul factory of **Jam and Lewis** (see next month's FACE) ■■ **Falls The Shadow**, at London's Hayward Gallery until June 30, collects new and recent works from some 30 British and European artists including **Georg Baselitz**, **Richard Long**, **Markus Lupertz** and **Gilbert & George**. Some of it so new that it will be created in the gallery ■■ **Baselitz** and **Lupertz** also figure in **New German Painting** — at Manchester's Cornerhouse centre until May 18 ■■ **Black Britain** support John Lydon's 1986-version **PiL** on a 16-town UK tour through May ■■ Jazz DJ **Paul Murphy** ups his public profile with pre-modern jazz and R&B at new club **The Purple Pit** (named after the nightclub in *The Nutty Professor*). It's at Camden's Electric Ballroom, Fridays from May 2 ■■ Quickies: a new Kathy Acker, title **Don Quixote**, and a new Thomas M. Disch, **The Businessman: A Tale Of Terror** (both from Paladin); a smart new **Woodhouse** shop, in Lynne Franks' old office in Long Acre; and a new Mont Blanc pen, the poser-friendly **Leonardo** ballpoint ■■ **Perrier With A Twist** is the traditional fizzy stuff laced with either lemon or lime. Smells like washing up liquid, says a Bulletin tester, but we like its zest. And anything Margaret Thatcher disapproves of is **OK by us** . . . ■■

Function versus form

In order to explore still further the relationship between function and form, two specialised registers of language – poetry and advertising – are looked at in some detail in the following section.

Poetry operates within a recognised register which takes language and exploits the accepted conventions and rules, often by breaking with convention and stretching the use of the language beyond the limits in normal communication usage. Poetry has a licence to break the rules and to force the reader to work extra hard to share the poet's message. It is valued highly by society, through the careful consideration of lexical choice and structure in this 'artistic' form of language.

Advertising, like poetry, is a recognised publi (one-way) register. Advertising uses language a specialised form which is an accepted publ mode. The reader participates in the process decoding an advertisement in much the sam way as the reader of a poem knows that they are taking on a specialised lingustic form. The British Airways advertisement (Fig 80) is ideographic in the way that poetry often is an the appeal is through the visual play on the language, not a verbal pun (see also Fig 82). This form is very carefully contrived and like poetry is highly condensed and draws upon other registers with the same artistic freedon It is far removed from improvised speech. The visible shape of poetry and advertising, are also very conventionalised 'visual registe and in many cases are integral components o communicating the message (Fig 81 and 82). These are extreme examples, but visual recognition is an expectation common to both genres.

Fig 80

uiet,

uick,

tran uil.

(You'll miss the Q's when you fly through Terminal 4.)

Right on cue, Terminal 4 at Heathrow opens on April 12th.

If you're flying with British Airways to Paris or Amsterdam, or any intercontinental destination, you'll find it uite different from other terminals.

First there's the sheer size of the place: 64 Check-In desks mean less congestion, less   ueueing.

This uni ue uality of calm continues all the way through to boarding.

Avoiding lifts, stairs and escalators you can uickly wheel your trolley direct from car to plane.

There's easy access by road, parking for 3,200 cars, a brand new Underground station and our own fast, fre uent bus service from Terminal 1 for passengers connecting from domestic flights.

In fact everything's organised to help you fly through Terminal 4 in double- uick time.

Any uestions?

BRITISH AIRWAYS
The world's favourite airline.

Despite the frequent outcries from critics, advertising enjoys a public popularity. The critics are usually voicing their objections to the ethics (or lack of) in advertising, the capitalist ideology, or the sexist/racism which may be perceived in some areas, or the so-called abuse of standard English. The general popularity endures because advertising appeals to the great majority through the element of intrigue, or puzzle/ambiguity which is often present in advertising. Ambiguity is a linguistic device to suggest a number of interpretations and is used a great deal in both poetic and advertising registers. Whether the puzzle is as intellectually pleasurable as a crossword, or visually pleasurable as part of the visual environment, they function in modern society as an easily accessible art form.

The 'pleasure/fun' element of playing games with language (as in advertising) is a universal characteristic of many cultures; in the Maya hieroglyphics quite deliberate puns are sprinkled in their texts. Poetry and advertising share a fundamental human characteristic of deriving pleasure from creative linguistic achievement. In poetry, the fun appeal is primarily in children's rhymes and limericks, where the linguistic ingenuity is easily recognised. 'Adult' or 'serious' poetry often has a more limited intellectual appeal amongst a minority readership, whereas advertising has to stay within the socially acceptable register of its target audience for maximum appeal.

Fig 81

Fig 82

Fantastic price reductions all this week!
Australiana & Travel, Cooking and the Great Outdoors, Hobbies and Professional interests in Management, Marketing, Sales, Computing and much more!

Special clearance of stock from the major booksellers in the City. 9 am till 4.30 (late Thursday shop).

Don't miss it!

MARKET PLAZA

BOOK SALE

Pantomime Poem

'HE'S BEHIND YER!'
chorused the children
but the warning came too late.

The monster leaped forward
and fastening its teeth into his neck,
tore off the head.

The body fell to the floor
'MORE' cried the children
'MORE, MORE, MORE

MORE MC

The most obvious difference between these two registers is the purpose of the writing (Fig 83). Poetry is an art form which is primarily an expression of one person's observations or feelings about something. This is communicated via linguistic form to anyone who cares to listen/read the message. Successful communication is not the paramount consideration for the poets who wrestle with their own command of the language to express an idea in the way in which they want to 'speak'. Writers of advertisements are seldom the originators of the need to communicate an idea. They are the agents who transform a message into language which is judged by the success it has with a clearly defined target audience (which may be measured in terms of the feedback through sales or attitudinal changes). Poets feel the need to compose but might never 'publish' in any form whatsoever, whereas an advertising copywriter is a professional composer of publishable words on behalf of a client. Poets often find a form of words which express ideas in a manner which becomes 'successful' by appealing to a wide audience. It is sometimes accidental and a bonus if success occurs during their lifetime. A professional copywriter must earn bread daily by composing lines which have to 'succeed'. Despite this wide difference of purpose, the techniques in manipulating the function of the language are very similar.

The advertiser's first problem of gaining attention in the media is very acute and with over 1200 messages a day being presented to the average reader in an industrial community extraordinary strategies have to be employed to secure attention. In most cases, as these messages are being absorbed through the visual senses, the pictorial image is a vital element in attention-getting. The combination of image and language to make the message is a frequent device but here we shall concentrate on the language message in its typographic form. In either case, many attention-getters are violations of the conventional rules and linguistic terms include spelling or grammatical deviations like the famous 'DRINKA PINTA MILKA DAY'.

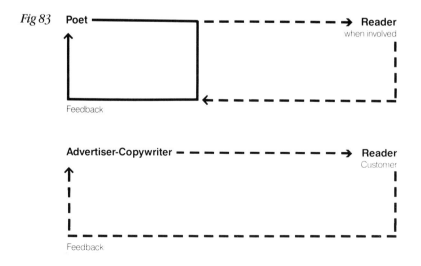

Fig 83

Poet ————————— → Reader
                              when involved

Feedback

Advertiser-Copywriter — — — — → Reader
                                      Customer

Feedback

Semantic deviation in the form of puns and metaphors are very often used, particularly in advertising headlines (which are the main attention-getters). *The Times* newspaper has run a series of posters which are based on puns:

'The prose without the con'

'Keep our wits about you'

'News real'

'Even if it's grim, we'll bare it'

'No juvenile leads'

Metaphorical substitutions, where the grammatical rules are broken, extend the pun upon words to quite extraordinary lengths which require considerable work on the part of the reader to understand the metaphor:

'Only two alka-seltzers ago' from an advertisement compares very closely to Dylan Thomas's 'a grief ago'.

A highly condensed linguistic form – compounding – is a particular feature of much modern poetry and is used to a great extent in advertising:

'The forest, rooted, tosses in her bonds
And strains against the cloud'

or 'Rose-cheeked Laura'

is easily compared to the 'so-many ways cheese'

or 'skin satin soft'

Compounding is deviation by putting together words which cannot normally be related to each other, and requires considerable inventive interpretation based on cultural knowledge of a language. The new associations present new concepts from words known in another context. But one way in which new words can be created is by compounding familiar parts of words and joining them with others, or applying suffixes to words:

'backsy forsy and inside out'

'The Freezer-pleezers'

New words may be invented in either register:

'And as in iffish thought he stood'

'He went galumphing back'

or

'Wonderfuel gas'

'The Forgettle'

Phonetic repetition (as in alliteration) can also be used in a creative interpretation of words which sound alike but are not the same in orthographic form: 'Mama mia, Rose is hia' (Fig 84). This is making a phonetic rhyme with a deliberate deviant spelling and playing upon the popular concept of a foreign language. A similar play with regional accent sounds may be found in poetry:

'Millery, millery, dusty poll,
How many zacks has thee as tole?
Vour and Twenty an' a peck,
Hang the miller up by's neck!'

Playing with words in the visual form, to ma[ke] them sound like another phrase in aural form[,] also alluding to other texts. The Barclays Ban[k] 'Loan Arranger (and Pronto)' (Fig 85) alludes [to] the stories of the Lone Ranger and his assista[nt] Tonto, and advertising and poetry often make allusions to other text 'histories'.

Fig 84

Fig 85

The shape of poetry is very important to the rhyme and metre. Conventional 4 line stanzas create a general text shape (Fig 86) which is a visual form distinct from that of continuous prose. The conventional treatment for body copy in advertising is just as formalised (Fig 87). It is distinctly recognisable as advertisement copy and was originated in order visually to emphasise the short sentences, as a means of encouraging the reader to carry on with the 'effort' required to read through to the end. The visual form is not accidental, and is as carefully contrived as is 'visual poetry'.

Less conventional modern poetry frequently makes each line important at it's own length. Many line endings are significant visual breaks interacting with the words, and advertising in all its display forms is equally concerned with the significance and impact which line endings bring to the enforcement of the message.

Poetry and advertising have many language characteristics in common; the layout or structure of the typography is also similar and sometimes there is much overlap in the form. However, despite the overlap *the visual registers are clear* and readers will normally have little difficulty in differentiating between poetry and advertising on sight.

Fig 86

Fig 87

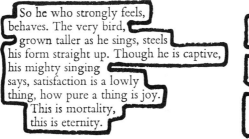

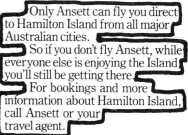

Ruder's 1967 publication *Typography* has much to say about writing and printing and the connotative qualities of the visible language, particularly in the opening chapters. The later sections on size and scale should be read by linguists who are analysing messages in the printed media. The examples are stamped with the uniformity of the Sans Serif typestyle and 'Swiss' layout, but the principles are relevant and easily transferred to more varied layout styles.

Again, numerous text books on typography have sections dealing with the 'appropriateness' and choice of typeface, but little of substance has been published on connotation. The most objective studies have been reported as articles in a few journals.

The most relevant periodicals which regularly have articles which are quite specific to the theme of language and typography are: *Visible Language* (USA) and *Information Design Journal* (UK).

The American journal has been in existence for many years and was formerly known as the *Journal of Typographic Research*. Readers will find numerous articles of interest from the many editions which have been published. The more recent UK publication takes a wider sweep at textural and pictorial communication and in the context of this and the preceding chapters, Volumes 1/4 (Mountford), 3/1 (Twyman, Rowe & Burton), 3/2 (Walker, Mountford), 5/1 (Walker/Smith/Livingston) are directly relevant.

Aural and visual literacy

The handwritten message is probably the simplest form of recording the visible language. Once the grapheme shapes have been learned, and the motor skills for 'joined-up' writing mastered for a faster cursive hand, very little technology is required. Marks can be made on almost any surface – sand, clay, wax, paper, brick walls, etc.

The teaching of orthographic skills in schools almost ceases at the 'joined-up' stage. Grammatical instruction continues primarily to enlarge the vocabulary and increase syntactical skills and comprehension. 'English' as a subject area is usually ideologically based upon the high points of human achievement in literature, to the exclusion of the main channels of communication in the industrial society with which most people have major contact.

Art teaching in secondary education concentrates on 'creative art' as practised by the great artists, and whilst it encourages those highly gifted with 'natural' drawing skills to perform better, it unfortunately frequently convinces those remaining that the visual arts are not for them. An over-simplification perhaps, but a basic visual literacy for all should be as important as basic numeracy or a basic linguistic facility.

The visible language is a part of the visual field, and a bridge to the verbal language. Access to knowledge of these domains is by separate avenues at tertiary level in education, or directly into professional careers. It is not surprising therefore that many public signs are produced by individuals and institutions which demonstrate incompetence in both language and visual skills. The sense, clarity and suitability to the purpose in our daily interchange via the visible language is dependent upon a much wider understanding of literacy.

It may help identify this broad field of public language usage to look at it as a kind of 'visible speech'. However, the metaphorical interpretation must be a very loose one. It serves only to present public communications in a different and more conversational perspective and to emphasise that there are more categories of language than 'spoken or written'. Public communications and the headlines of the mass media are somewhere between speech and written/printed prose. They have the visual sign system of the visible language and are channelled at a distance from the receiver. There is no spontaneous face-to-face interaction, but there are some similarities in signs attempting their 'turn-taking' in the babble of visible conversation pieces which are all seeking our attention in the environment. The visual prosodic cues, which are much more apparent in display text, prompt meanings from a contextual source which is derived from the same cultural heritage of the spoken language. The following tries to identify some of the territory to be explored by taking a few examples, and then suggests an approach to a more comprehensive visual analysis.

Example 1 – Advice to wearers of false teeth

The notice in a dentist's waiting-room (Fig 88) was drawn (approx 40 x 60 cm) by the receptionist, who probably extracted the wording from an official leaflet. Dentists' waiting-rooms frequently have notices on the walls which are often specially printed by dental health organisations on general matters of dental care, and 'local' notices in connection with that particular consultancy. 'Relaxing' reading material is generally available on low tables and usually consists of out-of-date magazines which have been passed on from regular subscribers. Information on the walls is typically non-prose and expected to be taken in very quickly. The 'audience' is captive for indeterminate periods and a little apprehensive about the coming ordeal.

This notice selects its readers with the heading (those who do not wear false teeth are not likely to read any further) and in view of improvements in recent dental practice, people with false teeth are likely to be of an older generation. The first sentence commands the reader directly '*have your* false teeth . . .', whereas the second imperative (2) and subsequent clauses are modulated by 'should' – 'often' and distanced from the first person. It is laid out in the list form, and despite being numbered 1 – 3, there are 6 items of information:

1 False teeth should be examined every 12 months
2 Examination is free
3 False teeth should be replaced every 5 years (pre-supposes that 'longer' causes problems)
4 NHS dentures cost £8.75
5 Exceptions for OAP and low income groups
6 DHSS claim forms necessary

Fig 88

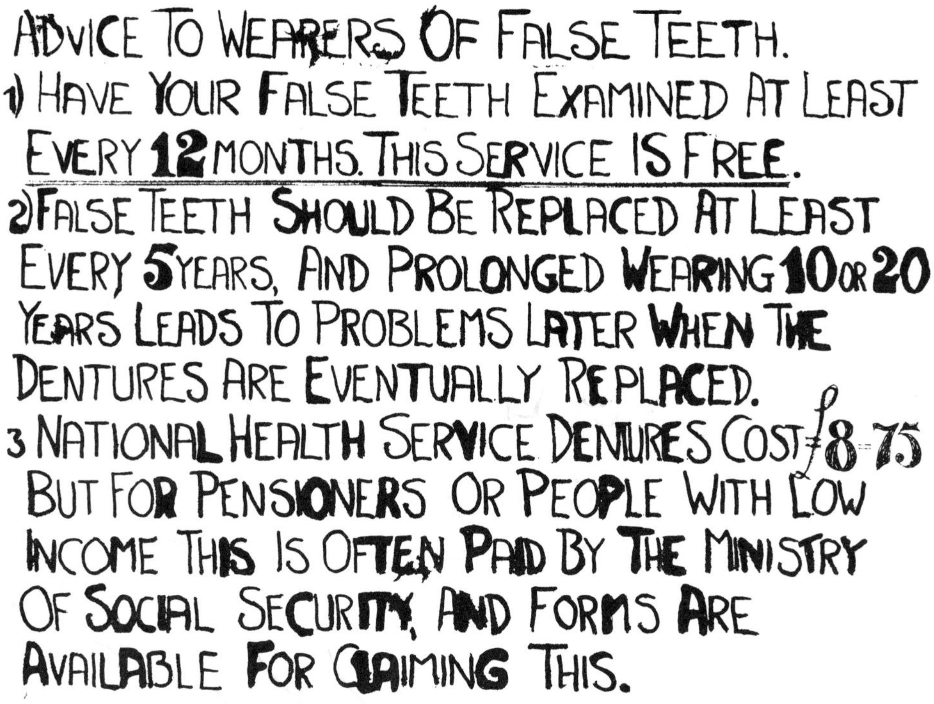

ADVICE TO WEARERS OF FALSE TEETH.
1) HAVE YOUR FALSE TEETH EXAMINED AT LEAST EVERY **12** MONTHS. THIS SERVICE IS FREE.
2) FALSE TEETH SHOULD BE REPLACED AT LEAST EVERY **5** YEARS, AND PROLONGED WEARING **10** or **20** YEARS LEADS TO PROBLEMS LATER WHEN THE DENTURES ARE EVENTUALLY REPLACED.
3 NATIONAL HEALTH SERVICE DENTURES COST £8.75 BUT FOR PENSIONERS OR PEOPLE WITH LOW INCOME THIS IS OFTEN PAID BY THE MINISTRY OF SOCIAL SECURITY, AND FORMS ARE AVAILABLE FOR CLAIMING THIS.

Visually there are many more problems of deviations in letterform and spacing which detract from the legibility and clarity of the message. The paper was quite absorbent and, in unskilled hands, the pen and ink scratched into the surface to spread and make some letters appear bolder than others.

It is worth noting that this visual extremity is not ugly or without purpose in itself. The poster (Fig 89) by the author was triggered by the analysis of the dental sign and uses the same apparently random visual characteristic as an 'attention-getting' aesthetic pattern for a jazz event.

Fig 89

Figs 90a to 90c demonstrate some of the stages in typographic conventions which could make this hand-drawn notice into a more legible and communicative message.

Fig 90a is an exaggeration in machine-made letterforms of the overall effect of massed capitals, with a random number of them in bold. The total effect is one of pattern and texture rather than a series of word shapes separated by clear word and interlinear spacing.

More realistically, Fig 90b shows the typographic equivalent at which the receptionist had probably aimed. There is very little distinction here between the degrees of importance in the message and it has minimum hierarchical structuring. Still in capital letters, Fig 90c shows the heading and 3 listed items separated by extra space which is an improvement on the readability.

Popular convention indicates that capital letters give greater importance to words but lower-case letters form more familiar word shapes and Fig 91 shows the message in upper and lower-case with more suitable spacing around the items and certain key words emphasised in bold type. This is probably as close to a 'professional' production as the original message could reasonably be taken.

Fig 91

ADVICETOWEARERSOFFALSETEETH
1)HAVEYOURFALSETEETHEXAMINEDATLEAST
EVERY12MONTHE'THISSERVICEISFREE
2)FALSETEETHSHOULDBEREPLACEDATLEAST
EVERY5YEARS'ANDPROLONGEDWEARING10or20
YEARSLEADSTOPROBLEMSLATERWHENTHE
DENTURESAREEVENTUALLYREPLACED
3)NATIONALHEALTHSERVICEDENTURESCOST£8.75
BUTFORPENSIONERSORPEOPLEWITHLOW
INCOMETHISISOFTENPAIDBYTHEMINISTRY
OFSOCIALSECURITY,ANDFORMSARE
AVAILABLEFORCLAIMINGTHIS.

ADVICE TO WEARERS OF FALSE TEETH
1) HAVE YOUR FALSE TEETH EXAMINED AT LEAST
EVERY **12** MONTHS. THIS SERVICE IS FREE.
2) FALSE TEETH SHOULD BE REPLACED AT LEAST
EVERY **5** YEARS, AND PROLONGUED WEARING 10 or 20
YEARS LEADS TO PROBLEMS LATER WHEN THE
DENTURES ARE EVENTUALLY REPLACED.
3) NATIONAL HEALTH SERVICE DENTURES COST **£8.75**
BUT FOR PENSIONERS OR PEOPLE WITH LOW
INCOME THIS IS OFTEN PAID BY THE MINISTRY
OF SOCIAL SECURITY,AND FORMS ARE
AVAILABLE FOR CLAIMING THIS.

ADVICE TO WEARERS OF **FALSE TEETH**

1)HAVE YOUR FALSE TEETH EXAMINED AT LEAST
EVERY **12** MONTHS. THIS SERVICE IS FREE.

2)FALSE TEETH SHOULD BE REPLACED AT LEAST
EVERY **5** YEARS,AND PROLONGUED WEARING 10 or 20
YEARS LEADS TO PROBLEMS LATER WHEN THE
DENTURES ARE EVENTUALLY REPLACED.

3) NATIONAL HEALTH SERVICE DENTURES COST **£8.75**
BUT FOR PENSIONERS OR PEOPLE WITH LOW
INCOME THIS IS OFTEN PAID BY THE MINISTRY
OF SOCIAL SECURITY, AND FORMS ARE
AVAILABLE FOR CLAIMING THIS.

Advice to wearers of False Teeth

1 Have your false teeth examined at least every **12** months. This service is **free**.

2 False teeth should be replaced at least every **5** years. Prolonged wearing for 10 or 20 years leads to problems when the dentures are eventually replaced.

3 National Health Service dentures cost **£8.75** but for **pensioners** or people with **low incomes** this is often **paid for** by the Ministry of Social Security and **claim forms** are available from the Ministry.

Fig 91 conforms to the current model of what a clinical piece of advice should look like and linguistically reflects the public authority 'register' which is typically expected. But it raises a number of issues.

Should 'official' language be used in this context where a slightly stressful situation is the norm? Is this register helpful to what is probably an elderly reader? Is the clearer visual presentation any better than the original drawn version, which at least echoed the human, personalised and sympathetic receptionist in connotative terms? Would it not be better to use simple, friendly language, clearly presented in a friendly informal hand? (Fig 92)

Fig 92

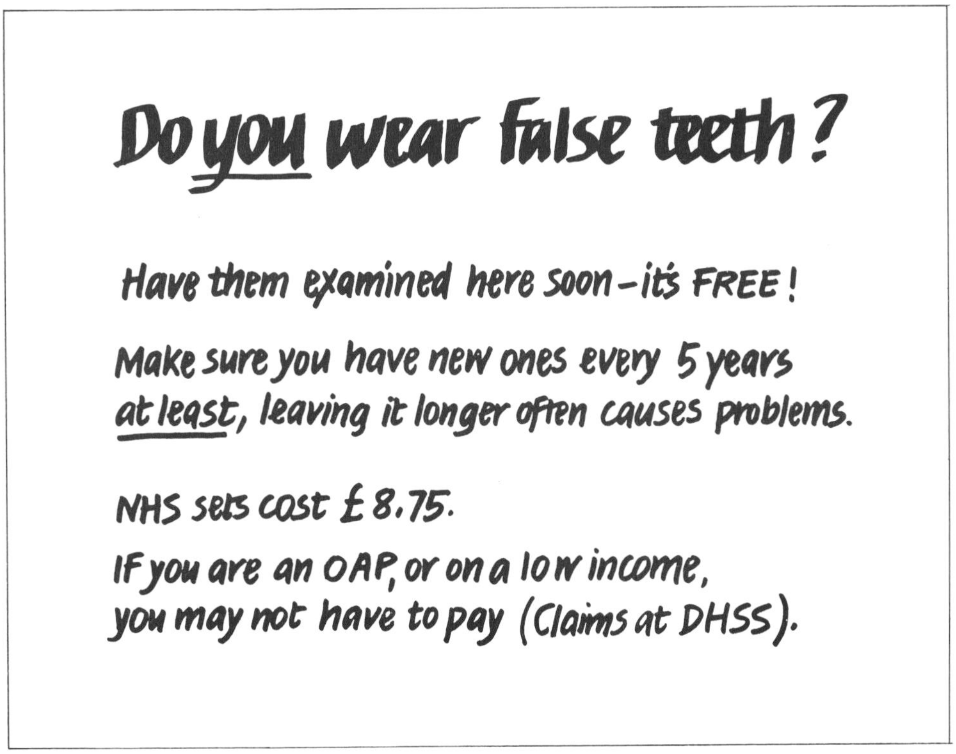

Do you wear false teeth?

Have them examined here soon – it's FREE!

Make sure you have new ones every 5 years
at least, leaving it longer often causes problems.

NHS sets cost £ 8.75.

If you are an OAP, or on a low income,
you may not have to pay (Claims at DHSS).

Example 2 – Yu can rede this

This A4 sheet (Fig 93) appeared in a doctor's clinic and embodies many of the virtues assumed in the above proposal in Fig 92. The heading is drawn in a crude 'dyslexic' manner which emotively identifies the subject matter and addresses directly the reader. As in many other examples of successful visual communication, it appeals through the direct visual word recognition route by deviation from the norm. This gains attention and is followed up with a question which is what the notice is really about – if you know someone who is dyslexic, they have some help to offer.

The language here is very simple and direct statement, question, answer. Anyone who is interested can find the addresses of people to contact. The hierarchical structure is clear. The handwriting is large and visible from a distance in the clinic. It is surrounded by white space which gives it clarity from its background. The question and answer lines are diminishing in size and the addresses are a collage of typewritten notes. In strictly 'legibility' terms the collage arrangement is visually disorganised, not well printed and abuses good typographical practice.

Fig 93

The associative code is close to 'hand-made', however, and brings a personal quality which reduces the distance between writer and reader. The only address in a sophisticated typeset style is the national address. The overall effect is one of urgency (from the child-like scrawl and collage/improvised technique) and offer of immediate help on a personal basis. There is the reassurance of the national organisation which imparts credibility of professional knowledge, and minimum waste of money on expensive printing.

Most of this 'extra-contextual' information is deduced from the visual presentation of which the unorthodox spelling together with the handwriting (shown full size Fig 94) is an essential feature. 'You can read this, do you know someone who can't?' read as prose, or spoken, would have far less impact.

Fig 94

Example 3 – Flower Show

Communication depends upon shared knowledge between the speaker/hearer, writer/receiver, and also the situation in which any utterance is made. The shared knowledge (which includes past knowledge of events and anticipated future with their implications), is a vast resource which is tapped by minimal utterances that strike the appropriate set of associative knowledge and concepts. If I say 'Kirsten phoned!' to my wife, she knows almost for certain exactly what her daughter wants to talk about, whether it has to do with something that has just happened or is impending, and will telephone her back. I do not have to say 'Your daughter Kirsten phoned about so-and-so, please phone her back . . .' etc.

The poster for the Flower Show (Fig 95) is a similar statement of minimum words, which in context makes full sense. It has no need to say where or which Wednesday or Thursday. It was used in a small market town in Devon which attracts a number of holiday makers. The locals would certainly have known about this annual event and would need only a reminder. The tourists, on probably weekly visits, would need to know the days of the week and little else. It is a clear, legible and totally communicative statement in 'irreducible minimum' language.

Fig 95

Example 4 – Fresh Fish

The context of this notice (Fig 96) is even more obvious in that it is stuck to the window of a fish (and vegetable) shop. The classic demonstration of redundant information is the shop sign 'Fresh fish sold here daily'. The argument proceeds: 'Fresh' is a dubious word to include as it might imply that it isn't, or wasn't, always fresh; 'daily' isn't required as the sign is only put out when the shop is open; 'sold here' is rather self-evident, as that is what shops are for; finally, there doesn't seem very much point in putting a sign saying 'fish' outside a fishmonger – conclusion, it is all redundant.

However, this argument misses the point. Apart from the concept of 'useful redundancy' which supplies the context that helps communication (it is estimated that 80% of the symbols on a page of English are redundant to the transmission of information), the purpose of this notice is not to inform, but to persuade.

The intention of 'sold here' is to remind the shopper that they do not have to walk any further, or waste time. 'Fresh', in addition to indicating that it is not frozen fish, is one of the more iconic words in English; that is, it is less arbitrary than most sounds and has a more direct association with 'tingle fresh' or the 'sch' sound used so effectively by Schweppes. The after-thought 'eg haddock, kipper, cod' are trigger words to assist the association of thoughts of eating particular fish – it is easier to conjure the specific image rather than an all-embracing set of alternatives.

It is hardly a clever piece of writing, but it is not a redundant notice. The propositional content is for the reader to make an 'impulse purchase' and although it appears to be a conventional statement of truth, it has much more to do with the conversational implication which the fishmonger might use with a prospective buyer, 'it's lovely and fresh, just imagine it on your plate, it's yours, here and now . . .' etc.

Fig 96

Example 5 – Farm Crossing

Many signs, like the traditional fresh fish sign (and conversation in general), work as messages by implication rather than a direct statement, like the Flower Show poster. Before moving on to deliberate implicature, it is worth considering the ambiguity, and sometimes nonsense, which is produced by accident. Competent use of language is almost an automatic assumption in society (and in much linguistic analysis), and when inabilities are exhibited they are often irritating, confusing, or funny. Despite the written/printed/painted word being worked on, edited, even lovingly prepared, it can still produce meanings which are not quite those which were intended (Fig 97). A farm crossing the road is only a mild example and in its environmental context it is not going to be misunderstood, but this kind of incompetence is often used as humour by comedians and advertisers.

A feature of public signs is their susceptibilit to 'added' comment in the form of graffiti. As in conversation, utterances can be taken out of context by other speakers, or given a different implication. The seaside fortune-te (Fig 98) was aptly teased with the one word 'unforeseen' added to the message.

Fig 97

Fig 98

A sign often seen around holes in the road (Fig 99) which appears to be a straight directive and of minimum orthography sets up a number of extra implications. Ostensibly it means that there might be gas or other inflammable substances which have been exposed, and a lighted cigarette or match may cause an explosion. It does not say 'danger'. The warning 'danger' is not always heeded, human nature being curious and somewhat defiant of challenges to bravery. The No Smoking sign is very effective at keeping the curious away.

Similar implications are generated with the signs of danger where the word 'snake' (Fig 100) has been added. It is reputed that the famous American circus owner P T Barnum created a fictitious creature called an Egress. He had experienced difficulty in one enclosure of curiosities because the customers would not move out (and make room for more paying customers), so he changed the sign saying 'way out' to 'this way to the Egress' and had no further problems. A more disturbing example has been quoted of the advice given by a New York policeman that if you're ever attacked in a hallway, don't yell 'Help', yell 'Fire'.

Fig 99

Fig 100

It can be seen that context is all-important in determining the effectiveness of an attempted communication. The speaker, or writer/designer, has an intention of communicating a message and may use all kinds of strategies to achieve that purpose, including false statements or deception. The listener/reader tries hard to work out the perceived message, but their understanding is conditioned by the pre-conceived notions, shared experiences and cultural beliefs they have in common with the sender. This culture, or ideology, is just as important in interpreting the visual codes as it is in the language codes.

However, the message and its context are inseparable. The originator is a captive of the culture in which the message is conceived and the form is predetermined by the environment factors which make up that culture.

Fig 101

Fig 103

Fig 102

The 'used car' signs (Figs 101, 102) are self-evident examples of messages which by their visual expression, indicate the context of their source. We do not have to be told under which of these signs the cheaper cars will be sold . . .

The cut-price lettering on the cut-price store appears to be reassuring to the customer who is looking for a bargain – in this case the lettering style is quite intentional (Fig 103).

Similarly, the deliberate invoking of a child-like scrawl as a fake message to Father Christmas (Fig 104), makes a powerful visual reinforcement of the message.

These signs rely mainly on the visual form to make their impact, other signs rely on the language structure. The direct command to drivers on the long and empty roads of Australia (Fig 105) is plain and straightforward in its visual construction. Its impact lies in the deliberate contradiction in the wording, and the invoking of another phrase which has become a famous slogan to stop drinking and driving. Similarly, the no parking sign (Fig 106) is based upon interpretation of meaning, without 'noise' interference from visual extravagance.

Fig 104

Fig 105

Fig 106

Ideology and design

Ideology may be defined as the set of unconscious values and beliefs which provide frames for our thinking and which help us to make sense of the world. In speaking or writing or designing we cannot avoid these frames of reference which are embedded in our culture. The relationship between speech and thought is interlinked and well expressed in the saying 'How do I know what I am thinking until I hear myself speaking?' Not that everything we say or think is a conscious act and it is important to recognise that ideology is largely hidden within a culture and so are the forms of thought which underpin the social structure and preserve it.

Another important factor is the plurality of values and beliefs and the sub-set of ideologies which make up a culture. There is a complex web of sometimes conflicting ideologies within any culture and when a culture can no longer contain such conflicts the structure breaks down in a crisis of social disorder. The network of ideologies which are contained is constantly adjusting to refinements, adaptations and new ideas which may seek to change or influence established beliefs. The constant interchange of ideas – discourse – simultaneously reinforces those ideologies and incorporates variations which affect the nature of the ideology itself for regurgitation the next time round. It is a constant process of reinforcement or change and modification. When the change or modification is significant enough for us to notice it, we generally categorise it as being creative.

Language is not the only feature of communication in the media and there are many others relating to visual imagery which are just as wedded to cultural ideologies. It is not the intention of this book to delve into the very broad field of semiotics but to stay within the constraints of the typographic form in which the language is expressed. Designers of the message form are just as conditioned by their visual ideologies as are the writers. In this respect, 'conditioned viewpoint' is also an occupational hazard for the analyst and if we are to minimise this effect it is important to have an objective framework upon which we can unpack the hidden ideologies in examining 'who says what to whom with what effect?'

A suggested approach to analysis

For the majority of straightforward signs and notices, a commonsense approach to 'who-says-what', etc, like the examples in the preceding pages, is quite sufficient. There are, however, many times when more complicated messages are being transmitted and a more systematic approach is useful. The diagram (Fig 107) shows a number of stages which might be identified but it is important to recognise that any analysis involves a constant recycling and re-evaluation in a continual process. The complex elements which make up an item of public communication are interdependent and although they have to be dissected during analysis it is only by moving forwards and backwards from text to context that we can develop an analysis in greater depth by each step. Given the additions of a first-stage 'overview' to describe the item and a final stage for conclusions, there are three main areas concerned with the physical structure, the sociological context and the psychological states of the sender and receiver.

The structural elements are usually contained in the two main areas of visual and textual, the visual being the typographic elements with the various connotations which can be invoked by selection and creative distribution, and the textual being the vocabulary, grammatical form and general cohesion of the language and other references drawn in.

The social context provides both a culture context with all the sub-cultures and stereotypes which are present in society, and an ideological context which reflects the orthodox sub-ideologies and sub-texts that are held by that society. These are the 'histories' that are being referred to in the visual and verbal languages used in the structure of the design.

Just as complex are the psychological attitudes of the sender and receiver. How much ideology is shared and is expected to be shared between the sender and receiver, and how this dictates the shape of the message and the reaction to it, becomes crucial at the point of contact – when the message arrives at its intended destination.

Fig 107

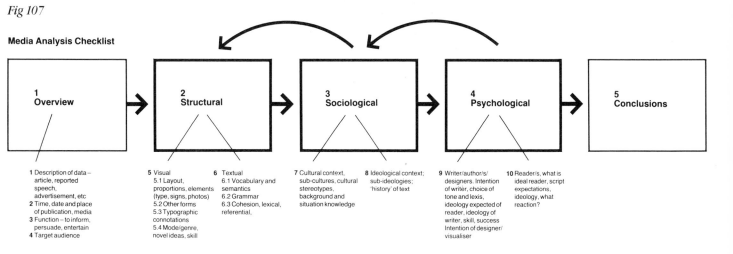

Media Analysis Checklist

| 1 Overview | 2 Structural | 3 Sociological | 4 Psychological | 5 Conclusions |

1 Description of data – article, reported speech, advertisement, etc
2 Time, date and place of publication, media
3 Function – to inform, persuade, entertain
4 Target audience

5 Visual
5.1 Layout, proportions, elements (type, signs, photos)
5.2 Other forms
5.3 Typographic connotations
5.4 Mode/genre, novel ideas, skill

6 Textual
6.1 Vocabulary and semantics
6.2 Grammar
6.3 Cohesion, lexical, referential,

7 Cultural context, sub-cultures, cultural stereotypes, background and situation knowledge

8 Ideological context; sub-ideologies; 'history' of text

9 Writer/author/s/ designers. Intention of writer, choice of tone and lexis, ideology expected of reader, ideology of writer, skill, success Intention of designer/ visualiser

10 Reader/s, what is ideal reader, script expectations, ideology, what reaction?

The advertisement for Shell (Fig 108) is used as a demonstration of the method in practical usage. The advertisement was used during the mid-1980s in *The Times* (UK) and has to be seen in that historical context (eg slightly before 'Green' issues became political currency in the UK).

1 An overview simply describes the item as a 3/4 page advertisement in *The Times* in the latter half of 1985. Its apparent function as an advertisement is to promote the good name of the company and is largely 'phatic' in that there is no specific product being sold directly; the company is simply keeping its name in front of the public and telling a story which reflects well upon its activities. The target audience is the normal *Times* reader who is generally middle-class and whose opinions are worth cultivating. It is also indirectly aimed at its own employees (and future employees) who might be made to feel proud to be part of a perceived 'good' company.

2 The advertisement is structured in a conventional visual format of the top 2/3 devoted to a display/illustration heading and 1/3 text in three columns. The display heading is unconventional in that it appears as a rebus in three lines of capitals with an image of a bee replacing the word 'be' in each case. This is the attention-getting device which engages the reader in a small game of de-coding the message.

The text and headline is set in a conventional roman letterform with connotations of tradition and authority. The same 'bookish' tradition is maintained in the columns of fairly large text type which have well indented paragraphs and are justified.

The visual structure of the text is dictated by the conventional short-sentence style of the language (referred to by Bill Bernbach as 'subject-verb-object' style). There are one-sentence paragraphs which emphasise the shortness of the reading task and are intended to tempt the reader through the text.

An informal and light-hearted conversational style is adopted, which reduces the distance of the reader from the unseen author and helps involve the reader in a more personal tone.

This is reflected in the colloquial phrases such as '. . . they wiped out the goodies and baddies alike . . . hum a sigh of relief . . . sprayed away . . . spared the innocent . . . under wraps . . ., etc.

The opening 'paragraph' is a list of insects (separated by full points) with the one oddity of the honey bee. This immediately ties in the heading/illustration with the text, and further examples of cohesion through the text are the continuation of sounds and ideas relating to the bee: '. . . hum a sigh of relief . . . bees were ecstatic . . . busiest, buzzing around for nectar . . contented, busy-busy bees . . . taken him under our wing . . .'

Despite the light tone, the subject matter is actually quite serious in that it describes the development of a new insecticide which the company has produced. The lexical references to the more serious subject of scientific research is another aspect of the cohesion of the text:
'. . . insecticides . . . bio-scientists . . . test-plot . new formula . . . field trial . . . long term result . . . project . . . research centre . . . environment effect . . . agrochemical . . . fungicide, pesticide . . . painstaking research . . .'

Fig 108

Flea beetles. Mealy bugs. Honey bees. Stalk borers. Cabbage stem weevils.

You're a common-or-garden human being, but you can probably pick out the hard-working honey bee from all those nasty, horrible pests.

Many insecticides can't. They wipe out goodies and baddies alike.

But now bees everywhere can hum a sigh of relief. Our bio-scientists have come up with an insecticide that can tell friend from foe.

The breakthrough came a few summers ago, on a test-plot of mustard. We set up some beehives, waited for the bees to gather pollen, then sprayed away.

Eureka. The findings showed that our new formula spared the innocents.

The bees lived to tell the tale. We were optimistic. The bees were ecstatic.

Over the next couple of years, we carried out one field trial after another.

We sprayed fields of flowering crops. We tried our insecticide on winter wheat, where bees forage for honeydew. We used it when they were at their busiest, buzzing around for nectar.

Each time, much to the bee keepers' delight, with the same long term result.

Contented, busy-busy bees.

This was no isolated, one-off project. Our research centre in Kent carefully studies the environmental effect of every new Shell agrochemical.

Be it an insecticide, fungicide or herbicide. (And more besides.)

Nor do we keep the results under wraps. We publish them in scientific journals for everyone, including our competitors, to examine.

Occasionally this may affect our balance sheet, but it's a bonus for the balance of nature.

As any honey bee, given the opportunity, will gladly confirm.

Our campaign to 'save the bee' took years of painstaking research. But if we hadn't taken him under our wing, who would have?

That is the question

3   The sociological context places this as a prestige advertisement for a multi-national company, easily recognised as such by the reader. The sign-off line 'you can be sure of Shell' confirms the status of this as an advertisement although it is instantly recognised as belonging to this genre.

The dominant ideology is about science. Shell is a company devoted to the products of science and until recently has been able to carry out research and present its products unhindered.

Science has been a taken-for-granted 'good thing' in modern society, preparing the way for progress, material comfort and the eradication of disease. This generalised 'good thing' has been called into question as the alternative lobby for ecological balance and natural foods and medicine has grown in support. The scientific specialist has been shown to make mistakes and infallibility is no longer assumed. Shell have tried to reduce the distance of scientific activity with all of its associated jargon by taking a light-hearted approach to tell a success story in simple terms.

4   The text presumes a number of concepts are shared by the reader: bees are hardworking and pests are horrible and nasty – bees are friends and pests are foes, beekeepers are delighted, etc. A small but significant sub-ideology is thrown in: 'occasionally, this may effect our balance sheet . . .' which presumes that profit is perceived as necessary and implies a philan-thropic attitude by the company. The penultimate paragraph presumes that bees were under threat without Shell's 'campaign' and 'painstaking research' where in fact it must have been similar scientific effort which provided the original threat. The final sentence 'that is the question' reads on naturally from the preceding paragraphs and cleverly refers back to the headline and triggers the Shakespearean quotation.

The puzzle of the headline has already been explained in the story but this final line is a firm bonus as a reward to the persevering reader. It adds to the puzzle pleasure experienced by the reader and, by making an enjoyable punch line, increases the goodwill towards Shell.

5   The advertisement is a good example in terms of the craft of advertising. It has a good visual puzzle to grab attention, a good fast reading middle story and a good end. It has projected the hidden ideology of 'science for the good of humankind' and incorporated enough of the ecological/environmental ideology to enhance the original all embracing 'good' science. The reader has consciously enjoyed the puzzle/humour and the educated references – both visual via the classical letterforms and layout – and to Archimedes and Shakespeare. In addition, and more contentiously at an unconscious level, the reader has acquired an association of the quality of Shakespeare with the quality of the company, and a reassurance of Shell's ability to further scientific progress while incorporating the balance of nature and reinforcing an orthodox ideology.

In this instance, the initial pun on words via a visual substitution, and the cleverness of the language in the text, was the main feature of this particular item and a conventional typographic presentation was probably the most appropriate format to structure the material. This and other examples could be milked further and there are many more examples which would offer a more creative and interesting set of cultural references which could be invoked by the visual transmission of the message.

Conclusions

There is sufficient evidence to show that the perception and understanding of the visible language is distinct from the reception of the orally transmitted language. The visible language is much more than a typographic system for spelling and punctuating the spoken language. It is more than is implied in the definition 'a system of visual signs for the temporal and spatial transmission of language'. Visual perception involves more than the ergonomics of legibility, it incorporates a deeply embedded culture-dependent interpretative activity. Just as linguistic communication succeeds only under certain conditions, the visual message-maker succeeds only when an attitude is intended to be conveyed and the reader recognises this attitude.

Chapter Four has shown that even without general visual images, the character of the letterforms and the way in which they are arranged within a rectangular frame imparts a 'personality' to the words and affects their interpretation. The body of knowledge that is evoked from a visual frame is just as important in providing an inferential base for understanding as in any language-based culture context.

Linguists have systematically extended their theoretical domain in the post-war period and progressively incorporated many other disciplines such as psychology, sociology and anthropology. They have often come close to the visual field in their analysis of language, but have almost always veered around it. Possibly this is because a coherent and comprehensive theory of semiotics has yet to fully emerge, but there is a wealth of linguistic material which is visibly and often intrusively displayed in the environment. Chapter Five has only begun to open the gate to this field. It is important that it is properly investigated.

The linguist Stephen Levinson observed that 'natural languages are constructed, so to speak, around the assumption of face-to-face interaction, and we noted how deictic terms can be misinterpreted when this face-to-face condition is not met. Analytical considerations may be quite helpful here to the design of crucial notices (eg on roads, or for the maintenance crew of aircrafts, etc) . . .'

Designers – and the general public – could do with all the help that linguists could give, where some notices such as fire-fighting instructions, hazard warnings, emergency exists, etc, are literally a matter of life or death.

Designers for their part, especially those who have to manipulate the visual form as typography, should understand the principles of language communication and apply these to the visible transmission of messages, rather than slavishly convert 'copy' into the latest visual fashion. Visual fashion – the style of delivery – is vital to the interpretation as we have seen, but it should never dictate the content of the message; it should serve to enhance meaning and make typography fully effective.

The work here has been derived from the media analysis carried out by linguists which, I have suggested, seldom makes reference to the size, shape and disposition of the language in the spatial frame. However, the standard publications start with Leech's *English in Advertising* which is sadly now out of print. If you can obtain a library copy, it is well worth it and incidentally it contains a very well-written summary of the development of advertising in the late nineteenth and early twentieth century. *Decoding Advertisements* by Judith Williamson draws extensively on Leech's pioneer work, as does Vestergaarde & Schroeder. Highly recommended is section 111 on advertising from *Language, Image, Media* (Davis & Walton), particularly Pateman's contribution on 'Understanding Advertisers'.

The Glasgow Media Research Group has made a systematic attempt at analysing news in the media and any of their publications are worth of study.

The increasing interest in communication studies will refine the techniques for analysis both the popular mass media and the design information material. It can be anticipated that the field work and literature will expand over the next few years.

The list of books which follows is by no means comprehensive, it provides the publication details of the books selected for comment, and offers a number of others which are generally recommended.

Author	*Title*	*Publisher*	*Date*
Aitchison, J	The Articulate Mammal	Hutchinson	1972, London
Aitchison, J	Language Change: Progress or Decay?	Fontana	1981, London
Aitchison, J	Linguistics	Hodder & Stoughton	1978, London
Barber, C L	The Story of Language	Pan	1964, London
Barthes, R	Image-Music-Text	Fontana	1977, London
Berger, J	Ways of Seeing	BBC & Penguin Books	1972, London
Bolinger, D	Language, the Loaded Weapon	Longman	1980, London & New York
Bolinger & Sears	Aspects of Language	Harcourt, Brace Jovanovich	1968, New York
Chipper, A	Persuade Me!	Longman Cheshire	1981, Melbourne
Crowder, R	The Psychology of Reading	OUP	1982, New York & Oxford
Davis & Walton	Language, Image, Media	Blackwell	1983, Oxford
Ellis, A	Reading, Writing & Dyslexia	Lawrence Erlbaum	1984, London
Fiske, J	Introduction to Communication Studies	Methuen	1982, London
Glasgow Media Research Group	More Bad News	RKP	1980, London
HMSO	Design of Forms	HMSO	1972, London
Lakoff & Johnson	Metaphors We Live By	University of Chicago Press	1980, Chicago & London
Leech, G	English in Advertising	Longman	1966, London
Leith, R	A Social History of English	RKP	1983, London
Lyons, J	Language, Meaning & Context	Fontana	1981, London
McCrum, Cran, Macneil	The Story of English	Faber & Faber	1986, London
Morgan & Welton	See What I Mean	Edward Arnold	1986, London
Morris, D	Gestures	Triad	1981, London
Myers, K	Understains	Comedia	1986, London
Ogilvy, D	Ogilvy on Advertising	Pan	1983, Sydney & London
Olson, Torrance, Hildyard	Literacy, Language & Learning	CUP	1985, Cambridge
Richard & Schmidt	Language and Communication	Longman	1983, London
Ruder, E	Typography	Tiranti	1967, London
Spencer, H	The Visible Word	Lund Humphries	1968, London
Steinberg, S H	500 Years of Printing	Penguin	1955, London
Stubbs, M	Language & Literacy	RKP	1980, London
Stubbs, M	Discourse Analysis	Blackwell	1983, London
Tschichold, J	Asymmetric Typography (trans R McLean)	Faber & Faber (original 1935)	1967, London and Toronto
Vestergaarde & Schroder	The Language of Advertising	Blackwell	1985, London
Williamson, J	Decoding Advertisements	Marion Boyars	1978, London